SHOTOKAN MYTHS

松濤館の神話

THE FORBIDDEN ANSWERS TO THE MYSTERIES OF SHOTOKAN KARATE

KOUSAKU YOKOTA

横田耕作

First edition published 2010. Second edition published 2015. Third edition published 2020.

ISBN: 978-0-9982236-4-3

This book was printed in the United States of America.

To order additional copies of this book, contact:
Azami Press
1-765-242-7988
www.AzamiPress.com
Info@AzamiPress.com

Dedication
奉納

I dedicate this book to the memory of Grandmaster Tetsuhiko Asai (1935–2006), tenth *dan*, Chief Instructor, Japan Karate Shotorenmei (JKS). He was the greatest Shotokan karate master of all time. He was my last sensei and is the aim of my unreachable goal.

Kousaku Yokota Biography
経歴

Shihan Kousaku Yokota (横田耕作), ninth *dan*, is a professional *karateka* with extensive experience in various martial arts. With nearly sixty years of training in Shotokan karate (松濤館空手), he specializes in Asai Ryu Bujutsu karate (浅井流武術空手). His wide range of experience includes training in *kobudo* (*nanasetsuben* and nunchaku), in the art of ki, and in the breathing method by Nishino Ryu Kikojutsu (西野流気功術). He was a member of the JKA for forty years and then joined the JKS for seven years. In 2013, he founded his organization, ASAI (Asai Shotokan Association International [www.asaikarate.com and www.facebook.com/asairyukarate]), to honor Master Tetsuhiko Asai (浅井哲彦). Shihan Yokota travels extensively around the world to share the knowledge and techniques of Asai Ryu karate. In addition to this work, *Shotokan Myths*, he is also the author of *Shotokan Mysteries* (Azami Press, 2013), *Shotokan Transcendence* (Azami Press,

2015), *Karatedo Paradigm Shift* (Azami Press, 2017), and *Karatedo Quantum Leap* (Azami Press, 2018). *Shotokan Myths* has been translated into French and Portuguese. All of these works are available on *Amazon*.

Acknowledgments
感謝の言葉

Many people are responsible for making this book possible, some more directly than others. I want to extend my gratitude to all those who so generously contributed their time and experience to the creation of this book.

A word of appreciation is due to Phillip Kim, photo designer, and Oleg Syrel, both of whom are my students. Phillip helped me with the creation of the beautiful cover design as well as the photos in the chapters covering Tekki *bunkai*. Oleg is a model in the chapter on Hangetsu *kata*.

And, last but not least, to all my past and present instructors, a heartfelt thank-you for giving me the understanding and knowledge of this great karate style of Shotokan. As Master Funakoshi said, "Karate training is a lifetime endeavor." Master Asai used to tell me, "Take one step forward every day." I learn something new almost every day.

In the past, I learned from my sensei and my fellow practitioners. Today, my students are my teachers. Without all of you, my karate would not be where it is today, and this book would probably not have materialized.

Thank you very much to all of you.

皆さん本当にありがとうございました。
Minasan honto ni arigato gozaimashita.

Foreword

By Patrick McCarthy
Hanshi Ninth Dan
Director, International Ryukyu Karate Research Society
Brisbane, Australia

What I most enjoyed about the treasure trove of information which lies before you is the simple way its author, Yokota Sensei, delivers all there is to know about Shotokan karate. Born, raised, and trained in Japan, Yokota Sensei has lived and taught Shotokan karate in the USA for more than three decades. Familiar with all the published work about Shotokan, he believes that much of its history, technical and philosophical information is scattered, inaccurate and incomplete. With a warrior's spirit forged in the furnace of austerity, Yokota Sensei learned the old ways directly under the tutelage of the late Master Asai Tetsuhiko.

In the spirit of *bunburyodo* (文武両道, 'the pen and the sword'), Yokota is a scholar warrior wielding a sword of simplicity to deliver a time-honored message. He clearly understands that the value of any chain is only as reliable as its weakest link. Likening Shotokan karate to a chain because of its strength and many links, Yokota believes that true mastery of this art is only ever achieved through the even balance of physical and mental training.

In other words, historical, technical and philosophical information must support physical training. When it does not, a noticeable imbalance occurs. Metaphorically speaking, by traveling further outside the physical art to study its nature, it becomes possible to penetrate deeper into its abyss. This important work links together such information and succeeds in delivering a comprehensive and easy-to-read study.

Bringing together a plethora of historical, technical and philosophical information related directly to Shotokan karate, Yokota Sensei provides straightforward answers too often glossed over or unaddressed. Moreover, the thought-provoking material covered in his book is simple and straightforward enough for beginners to understand yet diverse and comprehensive enough for experienced martial artists to enjoy, too. In short, the way the information is presented is sure to provoke all martial artists to rethink what they already know while challenging them to continue exploring their understandings in order to arrive at a definitive knowledge.

By sharing his thoughts and opinions in this work, Yokota Sensei builds a bridge across which the past is linked to the present. Providing a simple way to accurately pass on the history, technique and philosophy of Shotokan karate to the next generation of learners, he also pays homage to the legacy of the art while honoring the heritage of those pioneers most responsible for developing it.

Foreword

By Philipp Surkov
Country Representative, ASAI Germany
Göttingen, Germany
Born in St. Petersburg, Russia

Whenever more than two people come together, groups are created and, along with them, systems, rules and convictions. This applies to, more or less, every man-made system. Not only religions or political parties are affected, but also large athletic institutions as well as the small local club for martial arts enthusiasts around the corner. As time passes, the original ideals begin to dwindle away. This happens either because they were not passed down and recorded accordingly or because of the dishonorable character of a few influential individuals—people who use disinformation and manipulation to their own advantage.

Of course, there are also other factors that can lead to such changes. If such a system is 100 years old, the possibility of misunderstandings and false interpretations that get dogmatized is rather high. After 1,000 years, the original message gets lost almost completely. It is, therefore, very important that the responsible members of such organizations do their best to prevent disinformation and convey the principles as clearly and truly as possible according to the time they live in.

For me, Yokota Sensei is such a teacher. Through his blogs and books, as well as his work with ASAI (Asai Shotokan Association International), he fights for an ideal: a correct karate that can make the people and the world better.

Lying before you is the second edition of the book that opened my eyes several years ago and taught me to think critically in the world of karate, as well. Due to the easy understandability of the explanations, *Shotokan Myths* is perfect for you if you decided to immerse yourself into the depths of karate's history, philosophy and technique. However, not only beginners but also intermediate- and expert-level *karateka* should look into the book from time to time because the covered topics are multilayered; therefore, one learns something new every time he or she reads through it.

I hope that this book will have the same effect upon you as it had upon me since it spared me from making many mistakes and shaped my way of karate much more interestingly than before. I want to thank Yokota Sensei wholeheartedly for his continuous efforts and his lessons.

Foreword

By Philipp Surkov
Country Representative, ASAI Germany
Göttingen, Germany
Born in St. Petersburg, Russia

Wann immer mehr als zwei Menschen zusammenkommen, bilden sich Gruppen und mit ihnen, Systeme, Regeln und Überzeugungen. Das betrifft, mehr oder weniger, jedes vom Menschen geschaffene System. Nicht nur Religionen und Politik, sondern auch große sportliche Institutionen und der kleine örtliche Verein für Kampfkunstbegeisterte um die Ecke, gehören dazu. Mit der Zeit beginnen die ursprünglichen Ideale zu verschwinden. Einerseits weil sie nicht ordnungsgemäß weitergegeben und dokumentiert wurden, aber leider auch wegen des unedlen Charakters einiger weniger, jedoch einflussreicher Individuen. Diese bedienen sich der Desinformation und Manipulation zum eigenen Vorteil.

Natürlich gibt es noch viel mehr Faktoren, die solche Veränderungen herbeiführen können. Wenn so ein System 100 Jahre existiert, ist die Wahrscheinlichkeit groß, dass sich viele Missverständnisse und falsche Interpretationen einschleichen und dogmatisiert werden. Nach 1000 Jahren bleibt kaum noch etwas von der ursprünglichen Idee erhalten. Umso wichtiger ist es, dass verantwortungsbewusste Mitglieder dieser Verbände ihr Bestes tun, um Desinformation zu vermeiden und die Prinzipien zeitgenössisch, korrekt und so klar wie möglich zu vermitteln.

Für mich ist Yokota Sensei ein solcher Lehrer, der mit seinen Blogeinträgen, Büchern und seiner Tätigkeit in der ASAI (Asai Shotokan Association International) für ein Ideal kämpft: Ein korrektes Karate, welches die Menschen und die Welt verbessern kann.

Vor Ihnen liegt die zweite Auflage des Buches, das mir vor einigen Jahren die Augen öffnete und mich lehrte auch in der Welt des Karate kritisch zu denken. Aufgrund der Verständlichkeit der Erklärungen, ist *Shotokan Myths* perfekt, wenn Sie sich dazu entschlossen haben in die Tiefen der Geschichte, Philosophie und Technik des Karate einzutauchen. Doch nicht nur Anfänger, sondern auch die fortgeschrittenen Karateka sollten sich das Buch immer wieder zur Hand nehmen, denn die dort behandelten Themen sind vielschichtig und man lernt mit jedem Durchlesen etwas Neues dazu.

Ich hoffe, dass es auch auf Sie eine solche Wirkung haben wird, wie auf mich, denn es hat mich vor vielen Fehlern bewahrt und meinen Weg des Karate so viel interessanter gestaltet, als zuvor. Ich möchte Yokota Sensei für seinen unermüdlichen Einsatz und seine Lektionen vom ganzen Herzen danken.

Foreword

By Philipp Surkov
Country Representative, ASAI Germany
Göttingen, Germany
Born in St. Petersburg, Russia

Когда более двух человек заключают союз, образуются группы, а вместе с ними системы, правила и убеждения. Это относится, более или менее, к каждой системе, созданной людьми. Не только религии и политические партии, но также большие спортивные организации и тот маленький, местный клуб любителей боевых искусств за углом, числятся к таким системам. Со временем изначальные идеалы начинают исчезать. Это случается, либо потому что их неверно передали, или записали, либо из-за неблагородного характера редких, но влиятельных личностей, которые пользуются дезинформацией и манипуляцией ради своей выгоды.

Конечно есть и другие факторы, влияющие на такие перемены. Если такая система существует 100 лет, то велика вероятность того, что в нее прокрались некоторые недопонимания и неверные интерпретации, которые в последствии стали частью догмы. Через 1000 лет практически ничего не остается от изначальной идеи. Поэтому особенно важно, чтобы ответственные члены таких союзов старались не допустить дезинформацию и передавали принципы правильно, понятно и современным путем.

Для меня Ёкота сенсей именно такой учитель, который борется своими статьями, книгами и работой в АСАИ (ASAI [Asai Shotokan Association International]) за идеал: Правильное каратэ, которое может улучшить, как человека, так и весь мир.

Перед Вами лежит второе издание книги, которая несколько лет назад открыла мне глаза и научила меня критическому мышлению в отношении к каратэ. Благодаря понятности данных объяснений, книга “Мифы Шотокана” (*Shotokan Myths*) идеальна для Вас, если Вы решили нырнуть в глубины истории, философии и техники каратэ. Однако не только новичкам, но и продвинутым каратистам стоит снова и снова перечитать эту книгу, так как рассмотренные в ней темы многослойны. То есть каждый раз Вы научитесь чему нибудь новому.

Я надеюсь, что она повлияет на Вас, так же, как она повлияла на меня, потому что она сберегла меня от многих ошибок и сделала мой путь каратэ гораздо интереснее. Я хочу поблагодарить Ёкоту сенсея за его неутомимую работу и его наставления.

Foreword

By Donald Owens

Chief Instructor, All Shotokan Karate Association

Vancouver, Canada

Sensei Kousaku Yokota is the author of many articles on karate on the Internet. His articles have been thought provoking and interesting.

Sensei Yokota has an amazing history. He was born, raised and received his training in Japan. Sensei Yokota's first instructor was Sensei Jun Sugano, a very famous instructor indeed. He was also trained by the equally famous Sensei Tetsuhiko Asai. His pedigree goes well beyond this. For instance, he was a personal assistant to the famous Sensei Teruyuki Okazaki. Sensei Yokota's formidable knowledge and philosophy have made him a much sought-after instructor and writer.

Sensei Yokota has been living and teaching Shotokan karate in the U.S. for over thirty years, and it is this experience that has prompted him to write this book, *Shotokan Myths*. Sensei Yokota came to realize that, although there has been a lot of history and information published and written about Shotokan karate, in many cases, it is incomplete and sometimes inaccurate. It is Sensei Yokota's belief that valuable information should be passed down accurately and compiled in one place for easy reference.

In this book, *Shotokan Myths*, Sensei Yokota has extensively assembled a plethora of information relating to the historical, philosophical, technical and fundamental aspects of Shotokan karate. He gives straightforward answers to questions that anyone interested in the Japanese martial arts would like to know as well as more thoughtful and thought-provoking answers to questions that are more insightful. The material covered in this book is simple and straightforward enough for beginners to understand yet diverse and comprehensive enough for experienced martial artists to enjoy. The covered topics provoke all martial artists to think about what they know and challenge them to further rethink or explore their understanding to increase their knowledge.

Sensei Yokota has trained with many Shotokan karate masters of old. They had a profound impact on his karate training, and he brings with him this living history. By sharing his thoughts and opinions in this book, he hopes to pass on an accurate history, his own experience and the knowledge that he gained through his many years of training and teaching to the next generation of karate/martial arts practitioners.

Sensei Yokota believes that to study karate is not to just merely practice its physical movements but also to understand and respect its history and philosophy as well as to continuously challenge oneself mentally and intellectually. From my point of view, Sensei Yokota has accomplished what he has set out to do. He does not expect you to agree with everything he says but to have an open mind and not accept everything at face value. He expects you to look at things from an informed point of view and make your own decisions.

I highly recommend this book as I know each and every person that reads it will come away with a better understanding of Shotokan karate and will enjoy the way Sensei Kousaku Yokota presents it.

松濤館

PREFACE
初めに

Master Gichin Funakoshi, Founder of Shotokan Karate
(1868–1957)

As many people know, modern karate was introduced into mainland Japan from Okinawa only less than a century ago. Its introduction into the U.S. and Europe happened after World War II, or barely over seventy years ago. Despite such a short history, karate is now practiced by millions of people around the world, and this number is no exaggeration.

Considering that Japan is famous for exporting manufactured products such as electronics and autos, as a Japanese person, I am very pleased to see that a part of Japanese culture, karate, has made a big contribution to the world. At the same time, I am not fully satisfied with the current status of the karate world. There are several important issues, and one of them is the topic I am going to discuss in this preface.

I have been practicing karate for over half a century, and I have noticed that there are many myths and misconceptions about karate that persist even to this day. Of course, some are ridiculous, and most karate practitioners would laugh them off. A few examples of those myths are as follows:

- Fighting a big (police) dog is a *dan* examination requirement.
- A black belt must register his fists at the police station (like a gun).
- A secret technique called *three-year death* causes the victim to die three years after receiving it.

Unfortunately, there are other myths that are well known among practitioners and they believe most of them. Some of them are only misconceptions and may have little negative impact on karate practice or improvement of karate skills. On the other hand, there are others that would prevent practitioners from achieving true karate techniques.

I am fully aware that some of the points are controversial and expect some people to disagree with my opinions and explanations. I believe it is good to bring these points out in an open discussion where we can review them and think carefully about these important subjects. I definitely do not claim to know all or to have mastered all aspects of karate and martial arts. I am still searching for the truth and hoping to learn something new every day.

I credit my two instructors for my knowledge and understanding of karate. I am indebted to the following masters.

Master Jun Sugano (菅野淳, 1928–2002), ninth *dan* and former vice chairman of the JKA, was my first instructor at JKA Hyogo Prefecture headquarters in 1963 and was also the chief instructor of the Kansai region when I went through a *kenshusei* (研修生, 'trainee') period from 1981 to 1983. He shared much in-depth knowledge of Shotokan karate and its history, not so much in the dojo but more frequently in a bar that he owned where he used to take his assistant instructors for a drink.

He was a very well-known *karateka* in Kobe. I heard (from other instructors) that he had a very short temper when he was young and was often in fist fights. He lived in a town where a big yakuza group, Yamaguchi Gumi (山口組), had its headquarters. When they came across Sugano Sensei, they stepped aside and let him walk through, bowing to him as he passed by.

Sugano Sensei was big for a Japanese man, measuring 5 feet 10 inches and weighing more than 200 pounds. He probably did not need karate to fight. Though he had a scary face, he was a gentleman. He was respected and liked by all his students. It is unfortunate that he smoked and drank too much as those bad habits shortened his life. I was a member of the JKA for forty years—I had a lifetime membership—and, after Master Sugano's passing in 2002, I switched my affiliation to the JKS (Asai Sensei's organization).

Master Tetsuhiko Asai (浅井哲彦, 1935–2006), tenth *dan* and founder of the JKS and Asai Ryu karate (浅井流空手), was a world-renowned *karateka* and martial artist. He was the technical director (*shido bucho* [指導部長]) of the JKA for many years and then founded the Japan Karate Shoto Federation (日本空手松濤連盟 [JKS]) in 2000.

Asai Sensei passed away in 2006 from heart failure. He did not stop training or taking overseas trips even when he was seriously ill. He overworked himself, and his body could not keep up with his activities. He was one of the last samurai, and he died of and for karate.

He taught me many things that were beyond the knowledge of what I had learned when I was a JKA practitioner. His karate history does not need an introduction; however, there are several things that are not widely publicized, yet they are facts that affected his martial arts style.

White Crane Kung Fu

Asai Sensei lived in Taiwan for many years. While he spread Shotokan karate there, he took up White Crane kung fu from various masters. One of the kung fu masters with whom he exchanged techniques had a younger sister, a famous movie actress in Taiwan, and Asai Sensei ended up marrying her.

He practiced more than 150 *kata*. Some of them were created by him, and many of them came from White Crane kung fu. This is why his style was more circular and had a lot of open-hand techniques. You will also notice that body-spinning movements are common in the JKS *kata*.

Tenketsu (*Dim Mak*)

He studied *tenketsu* (点穴), an art of manipulation of the critical nerve points of the body. He knew the points of the body where he could inflict severe damage as well as paralysis, nerve damage, and possibly death. He said that, by applying pressure to those points, he did not have to depend on strength to make his blocks and attacks effective.

Weapons

He practiced many different weapons, including the *sai*, *tonfa*, *bo*, nunchaku, etc., but what he liked most was the nine-section whip (*kyusetsuben* [九節鞭]) as this weapon taught him how to use his arm like a whip.

Flexibility and Joints

Flexibility was very important to him. He spent a lot of time doing stretches to keep his flexible body intact. His body was like rubber, and it was not only flexible but also springy so that it bounced right back.

He also emphasized the importance of joint usage. He used to say, "You do not block with your forearm or wrist. You use elbows and shoulder joints." It was a difficult concept, but it made sense as he demonstrated his blocking techniques.

Relaxation and Ki

His moves were done in a whipping action, and this came not only from flexibility but also from total relaxation of his body. He also studied *kiko* (気功 [read as *qìgōng* in Chinese]), for his ki and breathing exercises, and his wife is a master in this art.

According to the National Qigong Association (NQA), "qigong can be described as a mind-body-spirit practice that improves one's mental and physical health by integrating posture, movement, breathing technique, self-massage, sound, and focused intent. There are likely thousands of qigong styles, schools, traditions, forms, and lineages, each with practical applications and different theories about *qi* ('subtle breath' or 'vital energy') and *gong* ('skill cultivated through steady practice')" (www.nqa.org/what-is-qigong-).

Even though there are many articles about Master Asai, there is no book that covers his experiences in karate and the martial arts in a comprehensive way. After the passing of Asai Sensei, Mrs. Asai was concerned that his name and contribution to karate would be forgotten. I hear that Mrs. Asai is currently making a movie about Asai Sensei and that she plans to write a biography about him sometime in the future.

Most of the ideas and concepts written in this book are based on the knowledge and wisdom I gained from these two masters as well as from my own personal research and investigation. I am responsible for all of the concepts and ideas.

I do not believe all my concepts and beliefs are correct. The facts I found in my research could be incorrect. I apologize to the reader if I have any incorrect historical facts or wrong ideas. I believe in never ceasing to learn until the day I die, so I am very happy to hear from any of my readers and to be exposed to any other facts or understanding that may correct my mistakes and help me understand karate better.

Introduction for the Third Edition

In the second edition, I wrote, "It is very difficult to believe that five years has passed since I first published this book in 2010." It is even more unbelievable that another five years has passed and that the third edition has now come out. This was the first of the *Shotokan* series. By 2015, I had completed the series with two more volumes: *Shotokan Mysteries* (2013) and *Shotokan Transcendence* (2015).

After that series, to my surprise, my writing continued. I started another series, which was *Karatedo*. During the last five years, I have published two volumes within that series: *Karatedo Paradigm Shift* (2017) and *Karatedo Quantum Leap* (2018).

I am also glad to report that *Shotokan Myths* has been published in both French (*Les Mythes du Shotokan* [CreateSpace, 2015]) and Portuguese (*Mitos do Shotokan* [Azami Press, 2017]), both of which are available on *Amazon*. I am currently working with translators in South America on a Spanish version. Demand is high, so I hope I can publish it this year, 2020.

The last volume of the *Karatedo* series is also slated to publish in the near future (maybe 2021). I have an idea for a title, but I will not disclose it here as it is not finalized yet. It will start, of course, with *Karatedo*. I think it will be a very exciting and educational book as the content is centered on the history and philosophy of the samurai. In each chapter, I select an interesting subject regarding the samurai or kenjutsu to show how it is related to or had an influence on *karatedo*. It needs a lot of research and investigation, so it has taken longer to complete than I expected originally. I thought I could publish it this year, but it looks as though it will slip into next year as I still have to write five or six more chapters.

I have many more ideas for future books after the *Karatedo* series, including one on Asai *kata*. There are nearly thirty Asai *kata*, but there are no *kata* books available for them. Many people have asked for such textbooks, but I have been delaying this project. I have a specific way of making such a textbook not only attractive but also more useful than existing *kata* books. To do this, I need to find a professional camera person who understands my idea as well as karate itself. This is a challenging task and is the main reason I have not produced such a textbook. Though it is challenging to find such a person, I am not discouraged. I believe the right person will appear when the time is right. I will keep you posted on this as it develops.

OK, I have written enough on my existing books and future plans. I hope you enjoy reading this third edition of *Shotokan Myths*. Finally, I want to thank you for purchasing this book. I always love hearing from readers, so write to me if you like it. *Osu*!

Master Masatoshi Nakayama, Chief Instructor, JKA
(1913–1987)

Contents

Dedication.....vii

Kousaku Yokota Biography.....ix

Acknowledgments.....xi

Forewords.....xiii

Preface.....xxv

Chapter 1 Kime.....1

Chapter 2 Hikite.....13

Chapter 3 Snapback in Mae Geri.....21

Chapter 4 Makiwara.....29

Chapter 5 Silent Kiai.....39

Chapter 6 JKA Bunkai.....53

Chapter 7 Begin and End with Blocks.....65

Chapter 8 Return to Starting Point.....75

Chapter 9 Mystery Kata Tekki Shodan Part I.....87

Chapter 10 Mystery Kata Tekki Shodan Part II.....101

Chapter 11 Hangetsu.....111

Chapter 12 Bujutsu or Budo.....131

Chapter 13 Contradiction in "Karate ni Sente Nashi" and "Sente Hissho"?..139

Chapter One
第一章

Kime
極め

Kime (極め) is a trademark of Shotokan karate. The reader will agree that perfect *kime* is what we dream of when we do the *oi zuki* (追い突き) or *gyaku zuki* (逆突き). Bang! Boom! Look at the *tsuki* shown below in the photo of Keinosuke Enoeda (榎枝慶之輔, 1935–2003). Yes, this is Shotokan.

Indeed, powerful punches and kicks are trademarks of Shotokan karate (松濤館空手). When you look at Shito Ryu (糸東流) *kata*, the performances look smooth and fluid, but the techniques look "weak." The Goju Ryu (剛柔流) *kata* have a lot of *neko ashi dachi* (猫足立ち) and *sanchin dachi* (三戦立ち), and, although the arm movements are circular, these movements, just like the stances, look short and do not have enough *kime*. (Note: I want to emphasize that I am in no way trying to bash any styles at all. I am simply comparing the general impressions of Shotokan and other styles.)

If the impressions above coincide with yours, then you may ask, "OK, so what?" Well, hold your breath; here is a shocking statement: *kime* (or, more precisely, encouraging *kime*) is probably the most harmful action for most Shotokan practitioners while training, particularly for beginners.

I am aware of the grave and controversial nature of my statement. However, I am convinced that all instructors and serious practitioners must be aware of and understand well this prevalent problem in Shotokan training. Despite the risk of being misunderstood, I dare to write this chapter as I believe this knowledge must be expressed publicly. So, please read on to capture the true essence of my statement.

I want to emphatically state that I am *not* identifying *kime* itself or having correct *kime* in your technique as a problem. If you are capable of producing good and correct *kime*, and you feel that your overall movements are fluid, then this may not be an issue. What I wish to convey is that the problem is the overly tense body that *kime* creates.

But, isn't *kime* a tense body? We remember some instructors explaining *kime* by saying, "In order to have *kime*, your entire body must be as tense as a bronze statue, like this," and they would demonstrate *kime* with a tense arm and a clenched fist extended in front of them as they stood in a very low *zenkutsu dachi* (前屈立ち). Their face would be contorted with tightly clenched teeth, and you could see the muscles around the neck pop out as they all tensed up.

Indeed, those instructors are successful, and many Shotokan practitioners do look like bronze statues. Haven't we heard or read the criticism by other styles (particularly by kung fu practitioners who love to categorize), claiming that we are "stiff"? We may just ignore them or their comments, saying, "They don't know the real power of Shotokan." But, can we really ignore their criticism when Shotokan is producing so many stiff- and rigid-looking practitioners? We could comfort ourselves by saying, "Let them talk. If we got on the floor, we could knock them flat on their faces with one punch." But, wait just a second. As long as Shotokan practitioners fight in noncontact competitions, no one will ever know for sure if your mighty punch would knock down your opponent. Or, would you want to challenge them to a full-contact, knock-down match?

Let's look up what *stiff* means in the dictionary. According to *Webster's Third New International Dictionary*, *stiff* is defined as "incapable of or resistant to being flexed or bent; lacking in suppleness—used especially of the muscles and joints; impeded in movement." Also included among the definitions are the meanings of "exerting great force; strong; of an energetic or powerful nature; forceful; vigorous," which include examples such as "a stiff west wind" and "a stiff left to the head." So, if one is stiff, his karate techniques can be powerful but may not be operating freely. Isn't this interesting?

I can see at least two serious and damaging problems associated with *kime*. One is the loss of power, and the other is the loss of speed in the techniques (punches, blocks, etc.). Additionally, the karate performance will not look smooth and natural but rather rigid and faltering. Let me explain these points further.

To get maximum tension (*kime*), the first and most important thing one must do is relax. The degree of tension correlates to that of the delta between tension and relaxation. In other words, the larger the gap between tension and relaxation, the sharper the *kime* one can achieve.

For the sake of argument, let's say that two practitioners will have the end result of a hundred percent tension. While one starts from relaxed muscles at twenty percent tension and then achieves eighty degrees of *kime*, the other starts from rather tense muscles at sixty percent tension and then achieves only forty degrees of *kime*, or half that of the first practitioner. This dull tension—though it may be a hundred percent *kime* at the end—will result in a pushing punch for the second practitioner rather than the sharp and snappy punch he wishes he had.

Now, all instructors and senior practitioners know this; however, beginners do not know how to control their muscles in a defined and intricate manner in order to balance tension and relaxation. So, they naturally tighten up all the muscles (total stiffness). We have witnessed this every time we see a white belt who moves like a robot.

This is all natural and expected. Remember when you learned how to drive for the first time? Do you remember how stiff your arms were as your hands were tightly wrapped around the steering wheel? How about now, after years of driving? By now you must be driving with one hand relaxed on the steering wheel and the other hand doing other things, such as holding a cup of tea, a mobile phone, etc., which I do not recommend at all. Naturally, you want to develop into this (relaxed arms) as you find that you can actually drive better and operate more freely. If you were a driving instructor, you would never say to a first-time driving student, "Tighten your arms to get the maximum strength to turn the wheel." You would say, "Bring your shoulders down and relax your arms."

Of course, the ultimate goals of karate techniques and driving skills are different. You are not trying to get *kime* in your driving; however, the fundamental concept of body or muscle control is still the mutual objective. By achieving fine muscle control, a practitioner can graduate from rigid, robotic movements to a higher level of fluid body movements.

I want to strongly advise all instructors to tell their students to relax as much as possible before making any body movements, including leg movements. You may object to the idea of relaxing the legs as we must always have strong stances. This is an interesting subject to discuss, but we will skip it here as we are covering the general concept of tension and relaxation for *kime*.

Premature *kime* resulting in a pushing punch is not the only problem. This condition will also slow you down considerably. Let's go back to the driving analogy. A pushing punch is the same as pressing on the brakes while stepping on the accelerator at the same time. I am sure you have seen an automobile in front of you with its brake lights continuously on even though it is still moving forward. Yes, that driver is stepping on the brakes and the accelerator at the same time. Although this action may be acceptable, it is not considered safe driving.

In karate, we do not want to have slow technique, half going and half stopping. We want to have a quick impact like a rocket slamming into a target. Have you ever heard of a rocket with a braking mechanism? Of course not. If that is the case, why do we need *kime* or braking in karate? Why can't we just shoot our fist out like a bullet and slam it into the target?

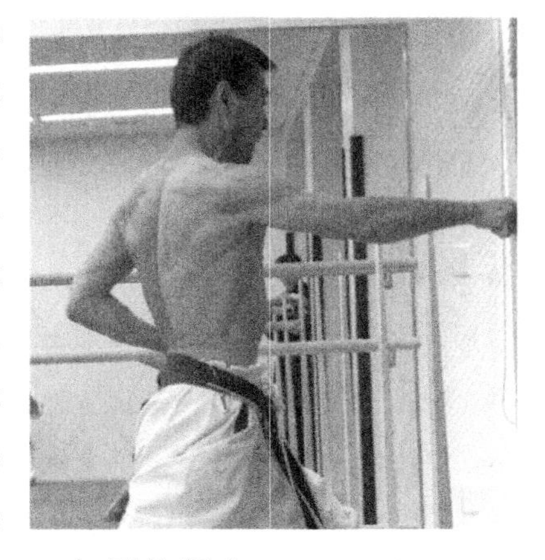

Well, a bullet is made of metal and can penetrate a solid target, whereas our fist is soft and light, so it does not cause a damaging impact when it is completely relaxed. Just imagine what would happen to your fist if you hit a *makiwara* with it in that relaxed condition. This is why you need to tense your fist but not throw it out like a bullet either. You need to use your body to drive the fist in like an explosive device in a rocket (see the photo of Mikio Yahara [矢原美紀夫, 1947–] above).

When we talk about *makiwara*, we tend to think of a piece of solid wood with a hard pad or a rope wrapped around it. This is the kind most advanced practitioners normally punch. There is also a softer one that can easily bend and has a soft pad. This one is typically considered to be for beginners. There is another way that advanced practitioners can use this soft *makiwara*, but we will not cover this in this chapter. I have related, however, a short history of the *makiwara* in Chapter 4, so you will enjoy that chapter if you are a *makiwara* enthusiast.

When you punch a *makiwara*, even if you only squeeze your fingers, this action will naturally tense the forearm muscles and will work as a brake, slowing down your punch. So, if your whole arm or entire body is tense, then the braking action that is created will be huge.

This is why *kime* must not last longer than a tenth, or even better, a hundredth of a second. *Kime* can be compared to the cutting edge of a sword—the sharper the edge, the better a sword can cut. In karate, a shorter tension results in a sharper technique. When *kime* is too long—say, one second or longer—the technique is no longer a sword but a wooden stick. When swung, a stick or a baseball bat can still hurt but cannot cut.

Then, why wouldn't instructors just say, "Use *kime* for a hundredth (or a tenth) of a second"? It is because a long tension has the visual effect and faulty look of good *kime*. It is like flexing one's upper arm muscles to show off the large biceps even though this itself is no proof of power or strength.

Having proper *kime* is indeed a technique in and of itself. Yes, it is a technique (actually a high-level one) just to be able to control the body in such a manner whether it is done with or without a karate technique in mind. Many instructors may object to my earlier statement by saying that they tell beginners to relax. They may be doing that, but that alone is not enough. What they need to do is go further and help their students achieve sufficient relaxation (or decrease their tension to the minimum level).

Beginners may say they are relaxed, but actually they are still very tense without even knowing it. An important job for any instructor is to bring down the level of tension before training starts and try to keep it down during the entire training session. This really is challenging for instructors as they could get a false sense of satisfaction from hard training, where all students sweat and pant. However, the most important thing for students to do in class is learn the techniques and how to improve them. If they want to simply sweat and get tired, they can always go to a gym and lift lots of weights. We must be honest and challenge ourselves to teach in environments where students can learn.

I must note that one factor that permits and actually encourages "long *kime*" is the popularity of tournament competition (both *kata* [形] and *kumite* [組手]). I decline to explain the details here. I consider it unnecessary as I believe most readers already know the relationship between *shiai* and long *kime*.

Accordingly, several known masters noticed the difficulty of relaxation and made some changes in their teaching and training. I would like to go over what the following three masters have tried and done: Shigeru Egami, Hirokazu Kanazawa, and Tetsuhiko Asai.

Shigeru Egami (江上茂, 1912–1981)
Shotokai (松濤會)

According to Egami's biography found on the *Shotokai Encyclopedia Karate-do & Martial Arts* website, Egami inherited the Shotokai organization at the age of forty-five after the death of Master Gichin Funakoshi (船越義珍, 1868–1957) in 1957. Here is a paragraph relevant to the point that I have been discussing:

> When you analyse the Karate-do that Egami developed through his years of studies, the mechanics of some techniques varied, the striking zone, the movements, etc. In broad strokes, the method became more fluid, more continuous. A strong emphasis on relaxation and the development of a perfect *kime*, focusing all the energy on one point.

That last sentence is right on target. In order to develop perfect *kime*, he believed that one must emphasize relaxation. "Focusing all the energy on one point" indicates the process of making a fist into a bullet that will penetrate the opponent.

According to the Japanese version of the *Nihon Karatedo Shotokai* website (www.shotokai.jp/en_about/en_teacher/en_egami), Egami started to change his training after the death of Master Funakoshi. It points out that he searched for the "ultimate punch with maximum penetrating power." If that was what he wanted to achieve, it was very natural that he came to realize that total relaxation is the key. The Shotokai seems to be a very exclusive organization, and its members do not believe in tournaments. They tend to stay away from cooperating with other Shotokan organizations (at least in Japan and the U.S.).

One interesting development from the search for total relaxation in karate by Egami is the birth of a new martial art, Shintaido (新体道). It was founded by one of Egami's students, Hiroyuki Aoki (青木宏之, 1936–). I do not have the space to explain what Shintaido is in detail here. I can only say that its techniques have much more circular body motions and relaxed movements like those of the Shotokai. I suggest that interested readers do some research on the techniques of not only the Shotokai but also Shintaido in order to broaden their knowledge and perspective.

Hirokazu Kanazawa (金澤弘和, 1931–2019)
Shotokan Karate-do International Federation (國際松濤館空手道連盟)

Kanazawa was a rising star of the Japan Karate Association (日本空手協会 [JKA]) in the sixties and seventies, but he left the JKA in 1978. He and his organization, the Shotokan Karate-do International Federation (SKIF), surprisingly, are better known outside of Japan.

It is well known that he practiced tai chi

and aikido to supplement his training. Even though there are several different training styles of tai chi (formerly *tai chi chuan* or *tàijíquán* [太極拳]), the best-known training is the slow-motion routines that groups of people practice together in parks in China. It is considered a soft-style martial art, an art applied with internal power. Obviously, he complemented the *hard-style* martial art of Shotokan with this soft-style martial art to supplement his training in order to achieve fluid movements.

He also picked aikido obviously to learn a martial art that focuses on throwing techniques. Aikido and judo have the same forefather, jujutsu, but it is natural that he chose aikido and not judo as the former has a similar *maai* (間合い, 'distance'), whereas that of the latter is a grappling distance. The techniques of aikido depend not on muscle power but rather on off-balancing techniques with a *maai* similar to that of karate.

As I took only a few seminars of Kanazawa's and did not have personal contact with him or his organization, these statements about him and his training are only my guesses.

Tetsuhiko Asai (浅井哲彦, 1935–2006)
Japan Karate Shoto Federation (日本空手松濤連盟)

It is very unfortunate that Asai passed away in 2006, but he left a great impression and influence on all Shotokan practitioners as well as those of other traditional karate styles. He is known for his flexible and limber body as well as his whiplike techniques. I am lucky to have received some personal instruction from this world-famous instructor.

Asai took up a Chinese style just as Kanazawa did, but he picked a hard style that focuses on external power, namely, White Crane, which is known as *hakutsuru ken* (白鶴拳 [read as *báihèchuán* in Chinese]), when he went to Taiwan in the sixties. He met his wife and her older brother while there. Asai's brother-in-law is a master of this style and is now in his eighties. Mrs. Asai has told me many interesting stories about the training sessions and technique exchanges between these two masters from two different styles.

Asai was a flexible person to start with, but from White Crane kung fu, he further learned how to use his arms and legs like a whip. To do this, he learned that his upper body must be totally relaxed to throw a strike and that his leg muscles must be totally relaxed to throw a kick. He also learned to control his muscles separately, as finely as possible, in order to gain the dexterity of the different parts of his body. Asai traveled to Europe extensively, so I am sure many of the Japan Karate Shoto Federation (JKS) practitioners in that region have witnessed the following feats.

He had such control of the muscles around his shoulders that he could move his shoulder quickly enough to cause an impact just like that of a straight punch. For him, a one-inch punch was an easy task. He said that the ultimate is the zero-inch punch with the arm totally straight and the fist touching the target. If he could punch with his shoulder, all he had to do was transfer the power to the extended arm.

He also showed the same power in his hips. He could knock you down with the whipping action of his hips when you tried to restrain him with a bear hug. It is obvious that, in order to carry out these feats, one's body must not be tense. Even in his later years, he spent a minimum of two hours every morning stretching and going through complex exercises to relax his muscles. You can see some of these unique exercises in a JKS video (VHS) in which Asai himself performs many *kata* and *bunkai*, including those of the JKA and White Crane kung fu.

As instructors of the twenty-first century, we are now obligated to have a better understanding of physiology and kinesiology. Let us recognize the importance of a relaxed body and put more focus on getting our body prepared for learning rather than on creating tension or generating power. Tension is a big obstacle for beginners and students who are trying to learn technique.

In the end, more relaxation will result in better *kime* with the additional side benefits of better body control and fluidity of body movements. By achieving this, we can proudly invite kung fu practitioners to our training and impress them not only with our powerful *kime* but also with our fluid movements just as Asai Sensei and Kanazawa Sensei did for other Chinese martial arts practitioners. In fact, the JKS and the SKIF both have dojo in Taiwan and mainland China.

In conclusion, I recommend that all *yudansha* (有段者, 'black belts') de-emphasize *kime* in their training and pay more attention to how to relax their body. Isn't it about time that we *yudansha* drop the robotic (rigid) body movements and begin to learn how to generate more power and more fluid body movements?

Chapter Two
第二章

Hikite
引き手

Asai Sensei executes a *jodan teisho uchi*. Notice the distinctive *hikite* with his left hand.

Is a good *hikite* necessary to execute a powerful punch? *Hikite* (引き手) is a Japanese word consisting of *hiki* (引き), which means ‘pull’ or ‘draw’, and *te* (手), which, of course, means ‘hand’. When I started karate training in the sixties, my first instruction was given by a *senpai* (先輩), and he showed me how to do *chudan zuki* (中段突き) from a natural stance. I’ll never forget him, Kato Senpai (加藤先輩). He was barely five feet tall but was as fast as lightning (as I remember him doing Enpi).

Anyway, Kato Senpai said, “Put your left hand out and set your right fist at your right hip. OK, that is where you start a punch. Now, draw your left fist to your hip very quickly and, at the same time, punch with your right fist, like this.” He executed an impressive *chudan seiken zuki* (中段正拳突き) several times in front of me. Though it looked quite simple and easy to imitate, I found that turning the punching fist was difficult, and so was drawing the other fist to the hip (*hikite*). He explained, “You need to pay more attention to the *hikite* than to the punching fist. The faster and stronger you draw your *hikite*, the faster and stronger your punch will become.” As it was my first day at karate training, his statement made a big impact in my mind.

A few months later, when I learned *gohon kumite* (五本組手, ‘five-attack sparring’), I had a problem with the *hikite* again. As we all know, after the fifth block the defender must throw a counterpunch. As the defender, I kept my blocking hand out (rising block, down block, etc.) as I delivered the counterpunch. My *senpai* said, “No! No! No! You need to do your *hikite* as you counterpunch. Your punch will be much stronger with a strong *hikite*.” I thought I had thrown a good counterpunch, but not doing the *hikite* was a big mistake that I had to correct. To be honest it was difficult not only because of my having to coordinate both arms but also because of my fear of lowering my blocking hand from *jodan age uke* (上段上げ受け) as the opponent’s fist was near my head. I feared that his fist might hit my face but I later found that the opponent was nice enough to hold his fist above my head.

I suspect that the kind of experience described above is very common for most people when they start karate training. I must emphasize that the correction and change forced by that *senpai* were the right thing to do, and I would have done the same thing in the same situation. When punching with a *hikite*, both arms move in opposite directions simultaneously. This process must become as natural as when both feet move in harmony when walking. If you try to walk with only one foot while dragging the other foot behind, it will not be a smooth walk, and the movement will not be natural. The walking mechanism is very natural to us, and the *hikite* mechanism can also become natural to the *karateka* (空手家) after a year of practice. After it becomes a part of your natural movement, you will not think too deeply about it, and you will have a powerful punch accompanied by a good *hikite*. At that point, you will have mastered a karate technique. This is great. We are all happy. Now I can almost hear you saying, "Well then, what is the problem?"

In this chapter, I am not disputing the importance of the *hikite*. I also agree that it should be taught and stressed to all *kyu* students. What I am objecting to is that this ingrained concept permeates the ranks of the *yudansha*. With the increased popularity of tournament *kumite*, where a visible *hikite* is almost mandatory to get a point, no one is questioning this. It is now a popular and unquestioned myth.

I began to wonder about this when I became a brown belt as I was exposed to the *morote waza* (諸手技, 'two-handed techniques'), such as *yama zuki* (山突き) in Bassai Dai and *morote zuki* (諸手突き) in Tekki. However, I did not ask my sensei about this as I was only sixteen then. Besides, in the competitions, we had never used or even seen those techniques (in the seventies and eighties). The scoring hand techniques were almost always *jodan oi zuki* (上段追い突き) or *chudan gyaku zuki* (中段逆突き) with a good or even an overemphasized *hikite*. So, it was not a big issue for me during my competition days.

I felt something was missing in *shiai kumite* (試合組手, 'tournament sparring'), so I retired when I was thirty-five. I quickly became serious about martial arts techniques. You do not see most of the *real* techniques in the controlled environment of *shiai*. To make myself clear, I am not bashing tournament sparring. It has its own place and merits, but it is a different world from the martial arts.

In a self-defense situation, you may not have the freedom of both of your hands, the space for a long stance, or the room for shifting. Besides, you may have multiple opponents. In those situations, you need to throw the first punch or execute simultaneous (blocking and countering) techniques. Those are the techniques that are shown in *kata*, and we all know that *kata* was created from the actual fighting experiences of the past masters. Also, in self-defense situations, using large motions in which both arms travel in opposite directions is not a good idea just as the long stances and *kamae* (構え) that we see at tournaments are also undesirable. Making inconspicuous movements is a must in a real fight.

As I reached for a higher level of technique, I came to realize that more defined control of the limbs is required to attain this. This is a concept of *kattai* (割体), which is pronounced like the joining of the English words *cot* and *tie* and means 'divided body parts' or 'segmented body parts'. This concept is very important and necessary to attain a high level of technique. It can be understood, maybe, in an analogy of beautiful music as played by an orchestra. Though many different musical instruments play their own parts and different sounds, these instruments are playing the same symphony as a whole. To produce high-level technique, the body must be used like an orchestra.

But, you may say, "Hey, I only have four instruments: two arms and two legs. How can I have an orchestra?" You completely underestimate what you have. The instruments you own are all of your muscles (more than 650 in the body), joints (elbows, wrists, ankles, knees, etc.), and bones (206 of them altogether). You have nearly nine hundred pieces of "instruments," and most of them are mobile (with the possible exception of the bones of the head), so you can see that the body is a grand orchestra. A simpler example can be found in other sports, such as baseball, football, basketball, etc. In the photo shown to the right, the pitcher must perform the final action or technique (in this case, throwing a baseball) by dividing the left and right sides of his body in order to carry out two different

movements.

A good example of a punch without the *hikite* is the one-inch punch. Many people may think the one-inch punch is a super high-level skill, but most *nidan* and higher ranks can master this technique if they are taught. Unfortunately, though, many instructors do not know how to do it. Actually, if you have learned how to transfer power through fine muscle and joint coordination, you can punch from a point at which the fist is already touching the target (i.e., a zero-inch punch or contact punch). I would need to have many pages in order to fully explain the mechanism of the one-inch punch and its technique, so, in this chapter, I will provide only a summary so that I can explain the basic idea.

To deliver definitive power in a one-inch punch (or zero-inch punch), one must know how to quickly shift the center of gravity from the rear leg to the front leg (i.e., the punching side). This requires fine movements of the muscles and joints of not only the legs but also the hips, backbone, and some portions of the upper-body muscle groups.

The punching arm is almost totally extended, so there will be almost no arm movement (including that of the wrist and elbow). Actually, the arm and fist are only the energy delivery tool (like a lance or a spear). There will be very fine and well-orchestrated coordination of the backbone, the shoulder joints, and the surrounding muscle groups to produce the punch.

With a slight roll of the hips and a small point of contact (one or two knuckles on the punching fist), one can generate a great amount of energy and produce a significant impact on the target. Actually, the arm and shoulder regions of the side that is not delivering the punch must be totally relaxed in order to generate the power on the punching side because this requires such fine coordination that it is best to utilize only the group of muscles that are needed to deliver the punch. There will be no upper-body rotation to produce power. Besides, there is no time for the *hikite* motion in a one-inch punch, and, more importantly, the *hikite* motion is counterproductive to this punch.

In *morote waza*, obviously there cannot be any *hikite*. We see many *morote waza* in *kata*, which tells us the past masters believed that *hikite* was not mandatory to deliver an effective technique. This can apply not only to punching techniques but also to blocking techniques. If you intend to disable an attacker's arm with a very strong block, you may add a *hikite*. However, you must also be able to deliver effective blocks without depending on the *hikite* or the leverage of a drawing hand. While you are blocking with one hand, it is very effective to use the other hand to simultaneously deliver a counterattack.

Another important point is that there is no value in holding a fist next to your hip. That kind of *hikite* is called *shinite* (死に手, literally, 'dead hand'), meaning that it is an empty shell. The hand needs to be up closer to the face to protect the face and head. At the same time, the hand is closer to the target and positioned for a punch.

You may be surprised to know that a punch can be thrown more quickly from a relaxed arm dangling straight down than from an arm positioned at the hip. Holding the fist at the hip forces some upper-arm and shoulder-region muscles to tense up, which will slow down the punch. A dangling hand can be whipped out very quickly and can deliver a lot of energy if a one-inch punch technique is used at the moment of impact.

So, I hope you agree that the belief that a *hikite* is necessary to produce a strong punch, block, or other technique is a myth. I also hope all instructors and high-ranking *yudansha* are training in a way that will improve their control of the various muscles of their body (*kattai*) so that independent movement of individual limbs becomes possible. Please remember that a body must become like an orchestra in order to reach a high level of karate skill. By being able to coordinate and move different parts (instruments) of the body in a skillful manner, our moves become a form of art just as an orchestra can produce a beautiful piece of music.

Lastly, I want to add that the original karate, maybe Funakoshi Sensei's teaching, stressed *hikite* for different, actually more martial arts-based, reasons. On Okinawa, there is a saying: "Make your opponent as a statue before you deliver a punch." What this means is that you are to get your opponent off-balance first in order to get the maximum effect from your attacking technique. There are three basic ways to get this effect:

1. Get the opponent off-balance.
2. Attack the eyes or the eye region to produce temporary blindness.
3. Wait till the very moment that the opponent starts to inhale.

I could address all three points in depth, but, for this chapter, I will only explain the first one. Obviously, if the opponent is off-balance, he will not be able to attack or even defend himself properly. How do you do this? You can push or footsweep him, or another common method is to pull the opponent toward you. So, the old teaching was to grab the opponent's wrist, sleeve, clothes, etc., and pull him toward you as you delivered your punch. Unfortunately, this concept was regrettably forgotten from the teaching, and only the word of *hikite* was left behind. So, some uneducated instructors started to claim that *hikite* was necessary to produce a faster and stronger punch. Of course, many students believed them, so this wrong concept became a part of the teaching syllabus. How unfortunate that the original teaching was lost.

Chapter Three
第三章

Snapback in Mae Geri
前蹴りのスナップバック

During your training in the past, have you ever heard an instructor yell, “More Snapback!” or, “Faster Snapback!” while you were doing *mae geri* (前蹴り)? Do you also remember that his yell put the stress on the *back* part? Yes, I am sure you have had that experience and most likely have heard those phrases more than a few times.

So, let’s look at how a snapback works. Take a look at the following formula:

$$F = ma$$

F (the force or amount of impact energy) is equal to m (the mass or weight) times a (acceleration). This simple physics equation proves the importance of the snapback. Since the mass is constant—your foot will not change its weight whether it is traveling forward or backward—the act of snapping back in *mae geri* could potentially double the acceleration, thus increasing the impact energy. So, it is easy to see that the influencing factor is a, or foot acceleration.

Therefore, it follows that the greater the speed of the snapback, the greater the impact of the kick. Does this make sense? So, your sensei’s command was right, and you owe your sensei a big thank-you for this instruction. Now you may ask, “Why are you making a big issue of this, then?” My answer is this question to you: “Is a kick without a snapback a bad or poor kick?” If you say yes, then you need to read on.

Is there a kick without a snapback that is considered a good kick? Of course there is. Have you not practiced *yoko geri kekomi* (横蹴り蹴込み) thousands of times? You may say, “Yes, but we snap back after *kekomi*, too.” You may believe that is what you are doing, but if you are executing *kekomi* correctly, believe it or not, you are *not* snapping your foot back.

You need to realize that the foot movement in *kekomi* is actually a pullback, which is different from the snapback of *keage* (蹴上げ). Again, if you are executing *kekomi* correctly, your kicking foot will stop as your leg is fully extended. If it doesn’t, then you have a *keage*. Therefore, even if you quickly pull back (not snap back) the lower part of the leg right after your foot stops, it will not add to your foot acceleration in the kick.

But, you may be thinking, *OK, that may be true, but my* kekomi *can make a great impact, maybe more than my* keage. Your observation would be correct, and that is exactly why I have written this chapter. Be aware that the energy your opponent receives from a *kekomi* is not from the impact alone but rather from the gross force. Here is the formula:

$$GF = mat$$

GF (the gross or accumulated force one receives from a kick) is the result of multiplying *F* (represented here as *ma*, which is mass times acceleration) and *t* (the length of time that the kick and push last). In *keage*, the impact time is minimal, so you want to increase the acceleration of the snapback in order to create a greater impact. In *kekomi*, on the other hand, you do not have the snapback (increased acceleration), but you can lengthen the kicking time by thrusting your kick (mainly with a horizontal movement of the hip region) to increase the gross force.

Let's see how it works. If *keage* is assumed to have an impact time of 0.1 seconds, and *kekomi* is assumed to have an impact time of 0.4 seconds (four times longer) but with an acceleration of only half that of *keage*, this will produce a gross force in *kekomi* that is twice that of *keage*. This shows you mathematically why your *kekomi* is more devastating and forceful.

Well, if that is the case, is *kekomi* then better than *keage*? As we all know, we cannot compare the importance of these kicks, or that of any other techniques for that matter. The character, or role, of *keage* is different from that of *kekomi*—I am sure I do not have to explain this point—thus, they are used differently, and they are equally important karate techniques.

So, the fuss I am making is about *kekomi*. We are very familiar with these two different kicks: *yoko geri keage* and *yoko geri kekomi*. But, think for a moment. Do we see *mae geri kekomi* (前蹴り蹴込み) or *mawashi geri kekomi* (回し蹴り蹴込み) incorporated into our regular training? No? Don't you agree that it is a bit strange that we don't? If you can say, "My sensei includes those kicks in our regular training menu," then you are very lucky. But, at dozens of dojo that I have visited or observed—though that number is limited and not at all exhaustive—I did not see these kicks in their *kihon* (基本) training.

You may wonder if these kicks are really that unpopular. Let me demonstrate that they are indeed not popular or standard. Karate Coaching (www.karatecoaching.com) is a popular and respected resource for online karate instruction. On their "Keri Waza" page (www.karatecoaching.com/kihon-keri-waza), they have a list of kicking techniques, which includes *yoko geri keage* and *yoko geri kekomi*, but we only see *mae geri* and *mawashi geri*. We do not see any other *kekomi* techniques listed under the kicking techniques. Hundreds, if not thousands, of karate practitioners must have viewed this website, but, apparently, no one has suggested the addition of *mae geri kekomi* or *mawashi geri kekomi*. Amazing! This means those two kicks have not been considered standard enough to be mentioned there.

Of course, there are other kicks, such as *ura mawashi geri* (裏回し蹴り), *gyaku mawashi geri* (逆回し蹴り), *kakato otoshi geri* (踵落とし蹴り), *kaiten geri* (回転蹴り), etc., that are not listed there, but those kicks can be classified as nonstandard. So, why ignore *mae geri kekomi* and *mawashi geri kekomi*? *Mae geri kekomi* must not be nonstandard if we find it in Unsu (雲手). Isn't this an advanced *kuro obi* (黒帯, 'black belt') *kata*? There is something very strange about this gap, and it is a mystery that these kicks are ignored.

By the way, you may already know this, but *mawashi geri* is a kicking technique that was added after karate was introduced into mainland Japan from Okinawa a little less than a hundred years ago, so it was not openly practiced on ancient

Okinawa. Therefore, it is natural that we do not see this kick in the *kata*.

But, did you know this other interesting fact? *Mikazuki geri* (三日月蹴り), a definite *kekomi geri*, is incorporated into many *kata*, such as Heian Godan and Bassai Dai. I will not quote from *Wikipedia* as the information there is not entirely reliable or accurate. However, it is true that it is a very popular site for finding information quickly; thus, I assumed karate information would be there, too. I checked the "Foot Techniques" section of the "Karate Techniques" article on *Wikipedia*, but, interestingly, I could not find it in this list. Do you not agree that this kick is rarely practiced in *kihon* training or used in *kumite* practice? Therefore, I conclude that *mikazuki geri* is another kicking technique that is not practiced in regular dojo training. No wonder this kick is not well remembered or respected.

Here is another very interesting question: did the ancient Okinawan masters ever practice *mawashi geri*? I am sure they did as *mawashi geri* is a very fast and useful kicking technique. However, they did not let other people know about this technique, which was secret at the time, as this would reveal their weakness. So, for the *kata*, they incorporated *mikazuki geri* instead of *mawashi geri*, the latter of which exposes the groin area too much.

The reader might then ask, "But, doesn't *yoko geri* expose the groin area, too?" You would be correct in your observation, and that is why the old Okinawan *kata* did not have *yoko geri*. As a matter of fact, the *yoko geri* in Heian Nidan and Heian Yondan were *mae geri* when the Heian *kata* were created in the late nineteenth century by Anko Itosu (糸洲安恒, 1831–1915), one of Funakoshi's instructors. Check out the Heian (or Pin'an) *kata* of Shito Ryu and the various schools of Okinawan Shorin Ryu. Their kicks are still done with *mae geri* and not *yoko geri*.

Now, let's get back to *mae geri* and *mawashi geri*. I would like to touch upon the very important subject of why *mae geri kekomi* and *mawashi geri kekomi* have been forgotten. The answer is that the popularity of tournament *kumite* has resulted in the neglect of these kicks. So, how did tournament *kumite* impart such an influence on kicking techniques? It is a complex and sensitive subject, but I will do my best to shed some light on this neglected matter.

There are two obvious reasons, and they both come from how our technique is judged in noncontact *kumite*. One is that a kick is judged as being effective (*waza-ari*) based not on whether or not it could knock down an opponent but rather on how it looks—this is the key word—to the judge. The other is that, generally, a knock-down will be regarded as a *chui* (注意, 'warning') or, in the case where the receiver is knocked out, a *hansoku* (反則, 'foul'). Some tournaments are rougher than others, and the *hansoku* rule may not be strictly enforced at these tournaments, but it is obvious that such a kick definitely does not score a point. A kick (or a punch, for that matter) in noncontact *kumite* must not have physical contact in order to score a point.

So, you cannot thrust your *mae geri* into your opponent's midsection or his chin to get a point. And, if you hold your leg up to maintain a *mae geri kekomi* without touching your opponent, he can easily grab your leg and take you down very quickly. For this reason (not because you want to have more impact), you are forced to snap it back, which means your kick must be a *keage*. Although it seems silly, unfortunately, this is a natural and unavoidable evolution.

Now you may ask, "Then, why is *yoko kekomi* widely practiced?" That is a very good question. Out of the three most popular kicks (*mae geri*, *mawashi geri* and *yoko geri*), *yoko geri* is the slowest kick because of the body mechanics in-

volved. Since it takes the longest time to execute, most competitors choose not to use it in tournaments. I have seen some competitors take a stance similar to *kiba dachi* (騎馬立ち) and try a Bruce Lee-style side-stepping kick. Unfortunately, this style results in a very visible kick and does not really work the way it seems to in Hong Kong movies. For this reason, we do not see *yoko geri kekomi* or *yoko geri keage* too often in tournaments. This may sound contradictory, but although *yoko geri kekomi* is not a popular kick at tournaments, it was not voted out of our regular training. It is amazing, but it is true.

Another big reason that *kekomi* is not popular in tournament *kumite* is the risk of getting a *hansoku* if a good *kekomi* is executed. I do not need to further explain the consequences of making contact to *chudan* (中段) or, more effectively, to *jodan* (上段). It is very effective to use *mae geri kekomi* in a *deai* (出合い) situation, but often that technique is called a *push*, and you will not get a point. So, competitors will use *keage* (in the strictest sense, a wrong technique) even in a *deai* situation. This kick will not knock the opponent down, but you will use it as it can score a point.

A *mawashi geri kekomi* to the side of head is very effective, but, again, there is no reason for a competitor to take the risk and try this kick if he can score a point using *keage*. First of all, a *mawashi geri kekomi* to the head is much more difficult than a *mawashi geri keage* to the head in terms of technique, so why take the chance of missing out on scoring a point? But, more dangerously, there is a risk of actual contact. In this case, you will knock your opponent down for sure and lose the match by *hansoku*. (As a side note, linguistically speaking, *keage* is the wrong word as it refers to kicking upward, but we will disregard this linguistic technicality here.)

It is interesting to note that in full-contact tournaments, *mawashi geri kekomi* is used very frequently, actually more frequently than *mae geri kekomi*, but this is not because the latter is less effective. I will explain below.

Full-contact competitors throw either *jodan* or *gedan mawashi geri kekomi*. It is obvious why they aim at *jodan*, but noncontact practitioners like us must know why *gedan* (下段) *mawashi geri kekomi* is also popular in full contact. In order to knock someone down with a kick—this is how you score a point—you need to really kick into the side of the knee or the thigh. A snap kick cannot do the job, so a *kekomi* must be used. The reason that *mae geri* is not used frequently in full contact is the close *maai*. The fighting distance is much closer than that of noncontact styles since *jodan* punches are not allowed by their tournament rules. The competitors actually get into a distance so close that they cannot even throw a fully extended punch, let alone a *mae geri*. But, if one is flexible, he can still throw a *mawashi geri* despite the close distance. In addition, even if an opponent were able to connect with a *mae geri kekomi* to *chudan*, he would not be able to produce sufficient speed and power from such a short distance when compared to *mawashi geri*, which has more distance as it is thrown from the side of the body. As a result, *mae geri* is not a favored technique in full-contact tournaments.

In conclusion, I want to emphasize that *kekomi* is a very effective kick from the traditional martial arts perspective and that *mae geri kekomi* and *mawashi geri kekomi* must not be excluded from our regular *kihon* and *kumite* training. I hope that not all practitioners will formulate their training to satisfy only the techniques needed in tournaments. There is a much broader range of real karate techniques out there. Wouldn't it be a shame if we allowed tournament rules to limit our training and hold back our quest to master these other techniques?

Chapter Four
第四章

Makiwara
巻藁

Michiko Onaga
Shijinbunkan Shorin Ryu

The *makiwara* (巻藁) is a true tradition of karate, and its training is a must for all *karateka*. It has been a fixture in karate dojo since its introduction into mainland Japan in the early twentieth century. We have seen pictures of Funakoshi Sensei punching one while wearing his *geta* (下駄, 'wooden clogs') or the photo to the left, which shows Yoshitaka Funakoshi (船越義豪, 1906–1945), one of Master Funakoshi's sons, doing *makiwara* practice. I have even heard that some modern-day sensei carry portable *makiwara* with them in their suitcases when they travel. The *makiwara* has been an important training tool in my karate life, as well. Let me explain how I got introduced to this traditional equipment in my first days of karate training.

At the first dojo I joined in the early sixties (Kobe Shotokan Karate Club), I remember there were several *makiwara* posts. Some were wrapped with straw ropes and some with softer pads. I also remember that those pads were no longer white or no longer had their original colors, whatever they might have been. The pads I saw were reddish black, covered in dried blood. It was obvious that my *senpai* punched these posts over and over again even when his fists were bleeding. My *senpai*, Kato San, once said, "Now look, my fist is so strong I can punch like this." He punched straight into a wooden four-by-four beam of the dojo. Bang! Bang! The beam shook, but he felt no pain (or at least did not show it.) Wow! I was very impressed. If he could punch that beam like that, he could easily kill me. Honestly, it really made me scared of this *senpai*, and he won my unconditional respect.

So, as soon as I was allowed to punch a *makiwara*, I started the tradition with all my might. My *dohai* (同輩, 'peer') Nakai (中居) and I punched the *makiwara* hundreds of times every day. After a year, Nakai had developed some very respectable calluses, but I was unable to. I was frustrated and thought I was not punching hard enough. No matter how hard I punched the *makiwara*, the calluses on my fists did not get larger. (I later realized that this was due to my skin's very rubbery and soft characteristics, which are actually very good for they allow me to be flexible, as well).

Despite not developing any respectable calluses, I kept up the *makiwara* habit for more than fifteen years. I must admit that the resonating sound made by hitting a *makiwara* in a dojo was euphoric, especially when the rhythm was so close to that of my own heartbeat.

I wondered if *makiwara* training was a true tradition and whether or not it had been handed down for many centuries. We know that the *makiwara* came from Okinawa, but we have little documentation to support its history.

I discovered one book, *Nanto Zatsuwa* (南島雑話 [photo right]), which is composed of five documents written by Satsuma samurai Sagenta Nagoya (名越左源太, 1819–1881). Nagoya was exiled to the Amami Islands, which were then part of the Ryukyu Islands. During his stay there, between 1850 and 1855, he recorded his experience in this book, and it's here that we find two drawings titled "Kenpojutsu" (拳法術 [photo below left]). As you can see in the top illustration of the photo, the Ryukyuan people seem to have used a post like the *makiwara* at least as early as the mid-nineteenth century. There are no other documents about the *makiwara* or its origin. However, by studying the history of Okinawa, one can guess where it came from.

Until 1609, Okinawa (沖縄), or the Ryukyu Kingdom (琉球王国), was independent. In April of that year, it was invaded by the Shimazu Clan (島津氏) of the Satsuma Domain (薩摩藩) of Kyushu (九州), Japan's southernmost island. The Shimazu sent more than 3,000 fully armored samurai for the invasion, and, given that no iron ore is produced on the Ryukyu Islands, which made swords almost nonexistent there, the Okinawans were no match.

Though recognized as an independent kingdom, the islands were referred to as a province of Japan. In 1879, Japan declared its intention to annex the Ryukyu Kingdom, and the latter became known as Okinawa Prefecture (沖縄県) by the Meiji (明治) government.

One interesting policy that the Shimazu introduced during the occupation was a ban on sword ownership by the islanders. The distance between Kyushu and Okinawa was great (around 600 miles [1,000 kilometers]) in that period; thus, it was difficult to manage the island from afar. The Okinawans most likely showed a fighting spirit at the time of the invasion, so the Shimazu needed to make sure that the Ryukyuan people would not rebel (or at least discourage such an idea). Many historians believe that this policy against swords led to the further development of the indigenous martial art called *te* (手), which can also be read as *ti* (ティ). Many practitioners of Okinawan Shuri Te (首里手) believe that *te* existed before the seventeenth century but that it became both deadlier and more secretive after the Shimazu occupation.

Another interesting thing we must pay attention to is the Shimazu's unique style of kenjutsu (剣術) called *Jigen Ryu* (示現流). Jigen Ryu is a very unique style as it is known for its emphasis on the first strike. In addition, Jigen Ryu teachings state that a second strike is not even to be considered. Now, doesn't this teaching sound similar to the idea of our *ikken hissatsu* (一拳必殺)? Interesting, isn't it?

But, the interesting part does not stop there. One basic technique, called *tonbo no kamae* (蜻蛉の構え, 'dragonfly stance'), is to hold the sword high above the right shoulder. The attack is then done by running toward the opponent and then cutting down diagonally across his neck with a loud *kiai*, "Ei!" What do you think? Doesn't this sound like how we attack *jodan* in our *jiyu ippon kumite* (自由一本組手)?

What is even more amazing is that the main practice of Jigen Ryu is to use a *bokken* (木剣, 'wooden sword') to hit a wooden post that is held horizontally. With all these similarities between *te* and Jigen Ryu, I conclude that the idea of the *makiwara* came from Jigen Ryu.

It is probably true that many *te* masters tried to learn kenjutsu from the Shimazu samurai. One documented fact is that Sokon Matsumura (松村宗棍, 1809–1899) took Jigen Ryu kenjutsu and was an expert in it.

I suppose that the invention of the *makiwara* occurred sometime in the late seventeenth or early eighteenth century. I say this because, in the early stages of the occupation, the Shimazu samurai were most likely cautious about a possible rebellion by the Ryukyuan people. Thus, they probably did not allow them to practice any kenjutsu, and they did not practice *te* in public.

But, after the passing of, say, one hundred years, if the Shimazu realized that the Ryukyuan people were loyal and peaceful, we can easily guess that the sword ban and the martial arts restriction became lax. Obviously, during the period when the Satsuma samurai Nagoya visited Ryukyu, he found the local people publicly practicing *te* on the *makiwara*.

The historical perspective is interesting to learn, but I personally came to the conclusion that punching a *makiwara* is not only unnecessary but also counterproductive to my fighting skills. In other words, we *yudansha* do not need to have calluses on our fists to knock someone down, which has been proven by various experiments and *kumite* experiences. Actually, it does not take much power or speed to knock someone down if a strike or punch is delivered to the right spot with correct timing. I have witnessed a black-belt competitor knocked down by a light hit to the temple with an *uraken uchi* (裏拳打ち, 'backfist strike') in a *kumite* match. The guy was not expecting such a hit, so he just dropped like a puppet whose strings had been suddenly cut off.

We must truly understand one important fact here. The characteristics of the human body are totally different from those of wooden posts (*makiwara*) and punching bags. The reader may remember a scene from one of the old *Rocky* movies where Rocky got into a large freezer and started punching a big chunk of meat hanging from a hook. Even though he was characterized as a dumb or not-very-sharp boxer, Rocky had the right idea. One can get a much closer feeling of what it is like to hit a man's body by hitting a large chunk of beef than a wooden post.

How about the other fighting methods, such as Western boxing, kickboxing, and kung fu? Do those practitioners use the *makiwara*? As far as I know, none of them do. Some tae kwon do practitioners may have picked up this training method in Korea due to the strong influence of Japanese karate, but that would be more of an exception. We must ask why most martial artists do not pick up *makiwara* training.

I concluded that professional boxers and other martial artists must not consider the *makiwara* to be a necessary training tool. It is true that boxers wear boxing gloves, so they have fewer reasons to toughen up their knuckles. On the other hand, they practice with different kinds of punching bags. They definitely believe they need to punch at moving targets, and I agree with them.

In some styles of kung fu, such as Wing Chun (詠春), wooden dummies are very popular (photo right). The dummies have many branches (mock arms and legs) sticking out, and one uses them to practice blocks, especially those using twisting wrist and elbow motions. Wing Chun blocks from a short distance—one's arms are connected to those of the opponent—and frequently uses twisting motions to block or divert punches. These blocking motions are very different from those of Shotokan, which are farther distanced and harder hitting. The main purpose of this wooden dummy equipment is to learn how to handle and manage an opponent's arms and legs, although it can also be used for punching. Kung fu practitioners must not see value in *makiwara* training either.

Why, then, would only *karateka* persist in hitting the *makiwara*? One of the key factors is the noncontact style. In kyudo (弓道, '[Japanese] archery'), where the archer shoots an arrow at a stationary circular target (*mato* [的]), it is obvious that the archer cannot shoot an arrow at a real person. The same idea exists in karate as it is a noncontact martial art.

I must bring up an interesting point about kyudo. Competitions are still held in kyudo, but practitioners no longer compete for shooting accuracy as observed in Western archery. The competition is about the archer's accuracy in his postures and body movements according to preset manners. This concept is very similar to that of *sado* (茶道, '[Japanese] tea ceremony'). So, kyudo has actually lost the *bujutsu* part and retained only the mental or spiritual part (focus, concentration, empty mind, etc.) of the art. I have noticed in recent *kata* competitions that more emphasis is being placed on nice looks than on the effectiveness of the technique. In this aspect, I am afraid karate competition is shifting the same way as kyudo competition.

There is also an emotional factor experienced by *karateka* when they are engaged in *kumite*. Due to the noncontact rule, they feel they have to punch or kick something to prove that they can punch and kick. This is why *makiwara* practice can be very popular as this frustration can be easily resolved by punching a *makiwara*. The *karateka* can punch it very hard to prove that his punches are powerful and devastating.

I must also point out that having big calluses has become a status symbol for some practitioners for these signify that one is a serious *karateka*. Some proudly show off their callused fists. I personally cannot share that feeling as it is almost like a yakuza showing off his tattoos. Although I have calluses of my own—mine were actually developed not from *makiwara* punching but from push-ups using my fists—they are not too noticeable, and I try not to show them in public, especially when I am in Japan. If people see them, they will quickly recognize that I practice karate. Karate practice is my personal affair, and I do not want strangers to know about it.

We must remember and recognize that our opponent, a human being, is constantly moving in a very complex manner. Perhaps the most important thing a *kara-*

teka must learn is proper and accurate *maai*, which is dynamically and continuously changing. In street fighting, it is almost impossible to set oneself in a fixed *zenkutsu dachi* and take plenty of time to throw a powerful *gyaku zuki* at the opponent as one could in *makiwara* practice. The reader may ask, "Isn't *gyaku zuki* the most common or most popular scoring technique at tournaments?" This is true, but it is not because *gyaku zuki* is the most useful and effective technique in karate or because other techniques, such as *ippon nukite* (一本貫手) or *shuto uchi* (手刀打ち), are ineffective. It is simply because the judges would not easily grant a point for those other techniques.

So, do I think *makiwara* training is totally unnecessary? No. On the contrary, I believe there is a place for *makiwara* practice as I recognize that there are some important merits to this training. For beginners, it is good to punch something solid, such as a *makiwara*, in order to learn how to align the fist, wrist, lower arm, elbow, upper arm, and shoulder as one throws a punch. Correct alignment of the fist and wrist is especially important. I am sure many practitioners have experienced (with pain) that if their alignment is not correct, their wrist buckles when they punch a *makiwara*. Punching a *makiwara* also allows one to toughen up the knuckles, and this will help if one wishes to punch something hard, such as a jaw or a head. *Makiwara* training definitely helps in developing hip rotation and clearly shows if one is successful in generating power.

I am aware of the other benefits of *makiwara* training, such as improved balance, center of gravity, etc., and the variety of ways in which one can punch and kick a *makiwara*. I am not denouncing *makiwara* training totally. The message I wish to bring to the *yudansha* is this: it is about time that we graduate from this tradition and move forward to the next level of training.

Chapter Five
第五章

Silent Kiai
聴こえない気合とは

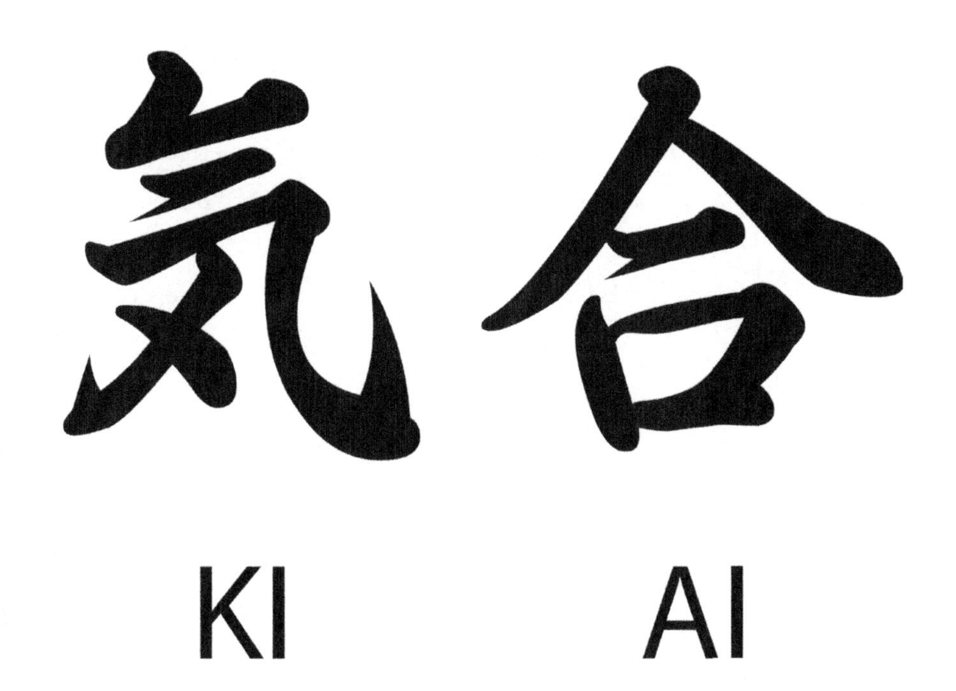

When you think of *kiai* (気合), what do you think of? If you are an old guy or gal like me, you probably remember that funny sound Bruce Lee would make. An amusing story from the past involves the men's aftershave called *Hai Karate*. If you remember this, then you must be at least fifty years old. This product was advertised on TV in the sixties and possibly in the seventies. Here is what the announcer said:

> New Hai Karate aftershave is so powerful it drives women right out of their minds. That's why we have to put instructions on self-defense in every package. Hai Karate, the brisk splash-on aftershave that smooths and soothes and cools. Hai Karate, aftershave, cologne, and gift sets. Hai Karate, be careful how you use it.

Then, there is a skit with a guy who has to fight off the girls who try to grab him after using this aftershave. Some of my friends must have believed that I needed this because, for several years, I would receive numerous bottles each Christmas. I really appreciated their genuine interest in helping me out, but I had to toss most of them because I could not have used them up if I had lived to be a hundred years old. Besides, I did not like the smell. I knew the aftershave would surely have driven the girls wild, that is, it would have driven them away.

There is also a very memorable incident involving *kiai* that I would like to share. I started karate fifty-two years ago (1963) in Kobe (神戸), Japan, and, thanks to the following experience in my very first class, I still clearly remember that wonderful day. I can vividly picture my *senpai*, Kato San (not the IJKA sensei), in front of me. As I mentioned in a previous chapter, he was barely five feet tall, but he was a towering figure to the new students (which included me, of course) as he slowly stepped up to us.

We were brand new, excited, and dying to learn those deadly techniques. He said very nicely, "You boys"—no girls dared join as it was thought to be too rough, but that was exactly the reason that I joined—"have to learn how to say, '*Osu*!'" As the reader may know, *osu* (オス) is a very convenient Japanese word that can be used to mean 'yes', 'no', 'maybe', 'I will try', 'right', 'sure', or whatever. It could mean almost anything, and we were always happy to use it as it allowed us to sound like tough karate guys. So, we all said, "*Osu*!"

The *senpai* then said, "What? I can't hear you!" So, we repeated with a louder voice, but that still did not please him. He then said, "You guys just don't have spirit. You are going to learn how to use a *kiai* today, and you will learn to show your spirit." He let out a really loud *kiai* that pierced through our bodies and sent shivers down our spines. Then, he smiled and said, "OK, boys, you will practice your *kiai* without stopping until I return."

We thought he would return in a few minutes, but he did not come back until the end of class, two hours later. We were yelling, "*Ya*!" or, "*Tou*!" or whatever *kiai* sound we thought was cool—we didn't know Bruce Lee yet. The *senpai*'s word was our command—plus, he was looking at us from the other side of the dojo—so none of us would stop. After thirty minutes or so, we started to cough and lose our voices. At the end, we could hardly make any sound at all. We left the dojo very quietly that day.

Incidentally, only one of the brand new students came back after that first day. That was the *senpai*'s way of separating the normal people from the crazy ones (me). My voice was gone for several days, but I showed up for training the very next day. I could only whisper on the following day, but my mother did not seem to mind as the house was quiet for a change.

Thankfully, the *senpai* did not ask me to *kiai* on the second day, but my training did not get any easier either. He now had me stay in *kiba dachi* for two hours while he kept saying, "Lower!" I knew I was too low when my legs would give out, I would fall down, and he would say, "Get up!" This simple but very long exercise went on like that, and I am sure you can guess how the rest of the Japanese way of training or breaking in the new student went. I am still not sure if that *senpai* really knew what he was doing or if he was simply too lazy to figure out a more sophisticated training method.

OK, you've heard enough funny stories about *kiai*. Now we'll address more serious stuff. There are many articles on *kiai*, and most authors have stressed the importance of doing it and explained how to do it. Some explain the meaning of *kiai*, while others show its relationship to breathing. If that is the case, then you may ask why I am writing this used-up and noncontroversial subject. Well, I am one of those people who do not like to take things for granted. So, here I want to accept the challenge and ask, "Is *kiai* really important, and is it necessary in karate training?"

You might say, "You must be crazy to challenge these things." Maybe you are correct, and I may fumble nicely with this subject. But, I think it is a good exercise to investigate instead of just believing something because many instructors and "experts" say it is so.

I wanted to see how the word *kiai* is defined in English, so I checked *Merriam-Webster's Collegiate Dictionary, Eleventh Edition*. It said, "The word you've entered isn't in the dictionary." I was not surprised to find that this Japanese word was not popular enough to make it into *Webster*. But, at the same time, I became a little curious, so I checked Japanese *Wikipedia*, expecting *kiai* to be listed there. Believe it or not, I could not find anything on it there, either. This may mean that the Japanese apparently do not make a big deal about this term.

This was indeed a surprising and unexpected finding for me, a Japanese author. I have about a hundred copies of Japanese books on martial arts, and the titles cover not only karate but also aikido (合気道), kendo (剣道), judo (柔道), jujutsu (柔術), *kobudo* (古武道), Okinawan karate, and *budo*. I have read them all but could not remember any books or articles on *kiai*, so I went through many of them, looking for it, but I could find only a short paragraph or two. Disappointingly, I could not find any chapter on this subject at all. That is why I decided to write a chapter on this subject for this book.

Does this mean this subject is a matter of common knowledge or that it has no depth, so there is nothing to write about? Is it too difficult to discuss the true meaning of *kiai* and its purpose? Or, am I just wasting my (and your) time after all by making something out of nothing? In order to find out, we'll need to go further. The *KaratebyJesse* website has an excellent article by Jesse Enkamp on *kiai*, "What Every Karate-ka Should Know about 'Kiai!'" With Jesse's permission, I've included some excerpts from his article here:

> First of all, what is *kiai*, exactly? To put it super simply; *kiai* is that scream you hear in most Asian martial arts (not to be confused with grunting).
>
> Although many people think *kiai* means something along the lines of 'battle cry' or 'spirited shout', the truth is actually a little bit different. A quick look at the kanji (Sino-Japanese ideograms) that make up the word should give you a hint as to what the term really means:

> Ki = energy
> Ai = join
>
> In other words, *kiai* is the convergence of your energy. Simple as that. Nothing mysterious or magical about it. Thus, when you scream *kiai*, you are not only "screaming" but more importantly compressing and delivering an instant release of your stored energy.

If you are interested in reading the whole article or other articles on Jesse's site, here is the URL: www.karatebyjesse.com/kiai-scream-meaning-purpose-why.

As I mentioned earlier, I typically do not refer to the information found on *Wikipedia* as it is often inaccurate. However, I will make an exception and share the main concepts of *kiai* that are described on *Wikipedia* here as I think they are good. Here are those four important concepts:

1. It is a short yell during a technique.
2. It can be silent, the sound just being an audible indication.
3. It can add power.
4. It assists with the ability to coordinate breathing.

Kata

All Shotokan *kata* (the twenty-six JKA *kata* specifically) have two *kiai* except for Wankan (王冠) and Meikyo (明鏡), which have only one. *Kiai* in *kata* are very distinctive, and they are a requirement in tournament *kata* competition. Have you ever wondered why there are always two *kiai* and not three or four? To understand *kiai* better, we need to investigate its history and learn the origins of this peculiar karate phenomenon. Here are some of the questions we need to answer as we walk through the history of karate:

- How were *kiai* done in ancient Okinawa?
- How did Funakoshi teach *kiai* and *kata* in the early twentieth century?
- Were the *kiai* mandatory then?
- Why do we have two *kiai* in almost all *kata*?

Did the ancient masters who created the *kata* strategically place two *kiai* in each one? All you have to do is observe the Pin'an *kata* (our Heian *kata*) of Okinawan Shorin Ryu or Matsubayashi Ryu to find out that this is not the case. I have found that the traditional organizations of Okinawa do the entire *kata* without any *kiai*. You may say that you practice Okinawan Shorin Ryu, and your *kata* have *kiai*

You have to realize that karate was reverse imported from mainland Japan back to Okinawa after World War II, so some of the newer Okinawan karate organizations may encourage their students to put *kiai* in their *kata*.

So, originally, Okinawan *kata* had no *kiai*. Why? It should be easy to answer if you think again about how the Okinawan *kata* were practiced during the seventeenth and eighteenth centuries, when all martial arts practice was prohibited. In a previous chapter, I mentioned that they had to practice their *kata* secretly in the middle of the night either in their backyard or in one of the remote graveyards. Could a loud *kiai* be implemented, or would it even be desirable in either of these situations?

So, you can easily imagine that *karateka* during that period had to practice karate very quietly. You may say, "But, Goju Ryu has very noisy *ibuki* (息吹き [photo below]) breathing as part of their regular training menu." That is true, but you must remember that Goju Ryu (founded by Chojun Miyagi [宮城長順, 1888–1953]) started in the twentieth century, after the prohibition had been lifted.

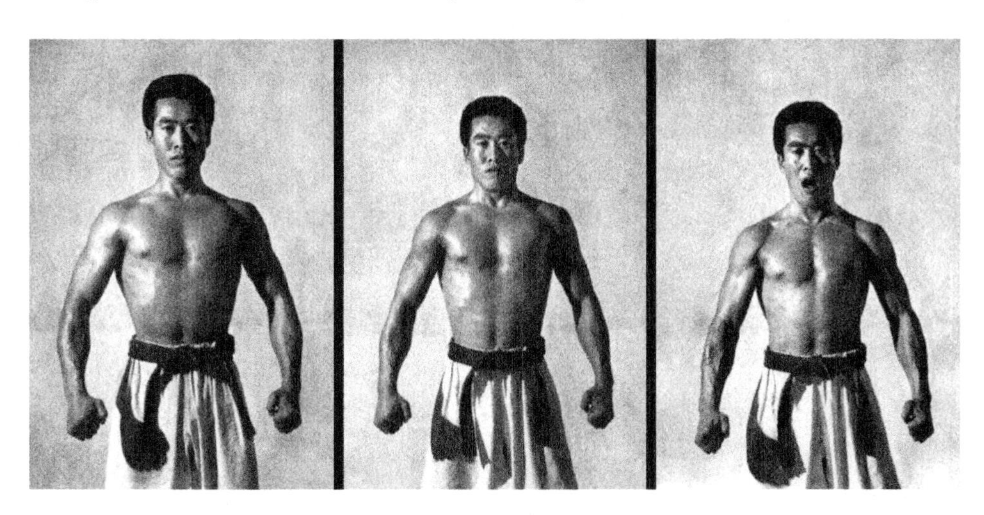

If the ancient Okinawan masters did not do *kata* with *kiai*, then when was *kiai* introduced into *kata*, and why the change? These are excellent questions, and we must find the answers. Not too many people have touched on this subject, but here I am happy to share my ideas with the reader as derived from my research.

Let us look at how Funakoshi taught *kata*. I have an old book of his called *Ryukyu Kenpo Karate* (琉球拳法唐手), which was published in Japanese in 1922. Unfortunately, no translated edition is currently available. In this book, he shows many *kata*, including Pin'an (Heian), Naihanchi (Tekki), Kosokun (Kanku Dai), etc., and describes the steps and the techniques, but there is *no* mention of *kiai* anywhere. I found this to be very interesting, and this was the starting point of my investigation on this subject.

Another interesting fact can be found in Shotokai *kata*. Only a few *kata* are available on the Internet, and I would be happy to hear from any Shotokai instructors regarding this matter. By examining the available video clips, I can see how Egami and his senior students performed familiar *kata*, such as Heian. Egami performed no *kiai* in his *kata*, and that was not a surprise to me as Egami did not like *kime* or tension. His movements are all stretched out and expanded. If he had done a *kiai*, it would have sounded like a *yaaaaaaaaaah*. But, I do not believe he added *kiai* in his *kata*. He was a devoted follower of Funakoshi, and I can easily assume that Funakoshi taught him *kata* without *kiai*.

Also, we must remember that the Shotokai fundamentally does not sanction *shiai*, so they have no need of tournament requirements and regulations as the JKA does. I hear, however, that some branches of the Shotokai are now getting more involved in some tournaments, so this tradition against *shiai* may be changing.

Let us next review *Karate Do Kyohan* (空手道教範 [Kobunsha, 1935]), which was written by Funakoshi and translated by Tsutomu Ohshima (大島劼, 1930–) in 1973, as this was the official textbook of Shotokan before *Dynamic Karate* (Kodansha, 1966 [photo left]) and the *Best Karate* series by Masatoshi Nakayama (中山正敏, 1913–1987) came out. Funakoshi listed nineteen *kata*, and Ohshima included notes showing where the *kiai* were to be placed on all but Jutte. Each *kata* had two notes and two *kiai*, but one thing that caught my attention was

that he inserted the word *customarily* into his notes. This word implies that the *kata* could be done without *kiai*. So, in the fifties, when Ohshima learned karate from Funakoshi, the guideline for *kiai* must have been given as a recommendation.

The JKA was founded in 1949 with Nakayama as one of the founders, and the books that make up the famous *Best Karate* series, written by Nakayama, have been the undisputed textbooks of the JKA. These can be used to identify where the *kiai* go as the word *kiai* is shown twice in each *kata*. So, after the JKA was established, the *kiai* seem to have become mandatory in *kata*. From close examination of all these textbooks, we can conclude that Funakoshi, at least in the early years in Japan, did not perform his *kata* with *kiai*, nor did he teach *kata* with *kiai*.

I suspect some changes must have occurred when he taught those university students in the 1920s and 1930s. Most of the universities in Tokyo had a *budokan* (武道館, 'martial arts hall') on campus, and all martial arts, such as kendo and judo, were practiced there. Just in case the reader is not familiar with kendo and judo, practitioners of those arts will surprise you with their noisy and frequent *kiai* during training. Those kendo and judo practitioners must have let out lots of *kiai* at the *budokan*, and the students of the karate club would have heard them.

It is easy to suspect that the karate students would have felt embarrassed as they made no noise while they did their shadow boxing. During those years, Funakoshi had them practice only *kata* and very little *kumite*. In fact, some of the students could not keep Funakoshi's rule that barred them from doing *jiyu kumite* (自由組手, 'free sparring'). I heard that, when he found out some of his students were doing this secretly, he actually resigned from his instructor's position at that particular university.

So, it is easy to guess that those energetic students wanted to let out a loud *kiai* to show their spirit. I suspect Funakoshi gave in as he did not want to suppress the energy of those young students too much. In addition, he probably thought a loud *kiai* was good for the beginners as they tend to hold their breath.

Karate is originally from China, and, after investigation, it's difficult to conclude whether there were *kiai* in the *kata* initially as we do not know the original Chinese *kata*. By studying some of the current Chinese *kata*, I found that some of them are practiced with *kiai* and some without, especially in tai chi and *bāguàzhǎng* (八卦掌). However, one thing I have noticed is that these *kiai* do not come in sets of two. I also found that the ways they deliver *kiai* are different. I will not go into detail with this subject as it is not my aim to do a comparison here.

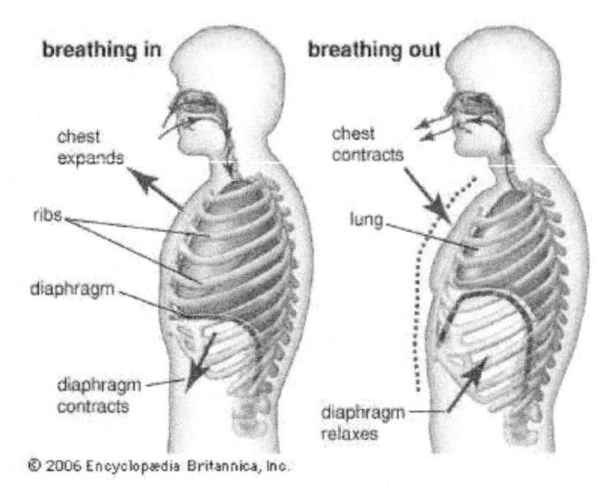

We still need to come back to the original question: why do the current *kata* have two *kiai*? Shotokan's origin is Shuri Te, in which natural breathing is practiced, so practitioners are supposedly expected to perform all the techniques without making any breathing noises. Unnecessarily holding one's breath is what happens with this training method unless the student is instructed on how to breathe correctly, and this is what we often witness among beginners.

But, this still does not explain why there have to be two *kiai* in each *kata*. I believe this came about when the tournament rules were originally made fifty-some years ago. If we put the historical evidence that I described earlier together with the fact that the JKA held the first All Japan Championship in 1957, the year Funakoshi passed away, it is pretty easy to draw the conclusion that the JKA firmed up the requirement of having two *kiai* in each *kata*.

So, this was originally created for tournament competition. But, why then did they choose two *kiai* instead of one or three? It's my educated guess that each *kata* has the Japanese concept of *omote* (表, 'front') and *ura* (裏, 'back' or 'rear'), or yin and yang (*in'yo* [陰陽]). So, the first *kiai* will end the front or first part of the *kata*, and the second one will finish out the back or latter part of the *kata*. Though the second *kiai* is typically at the end, there are a few *kata* that have an additional one or two steps after the second *kiai*, such as Hangetsu, Meikyo, and Enpi.

So, Nakayama, as the chief instructor of the JKA, was the person responsible for this requirement in the JKA exam syllabus and the tournament regulations.

Kumite

It is also a fact that loud *kiai* are encouraged not only in tournament *kumite* but also in regular *kumite* training. In fact, in a tournament, you probably need a good *kiai* to score the full point. If you are a tournament fighter, you may recall a match when you threw a good technique, but a full point was not granted because either you did not *kiai* or your *kiai* was weak.

Some instructors would say your techniques are stronger with a louder *kiai*. Is this really so? If this is the case, why do we not see boxers yelling loudly as they throw punches? I have watched many boxing matches, but I have never witnessed any of the fighters, including champions such as Muhammad Ali, Sugar Ray Leonard, and Mike Tyson, do anything like that.

But, you might say, "I have seen weight lifters and shot putters let out similar yells when they lift and throw." You are correct, but you must also evaluate and compare the fundamental differences between the techniques and physiological mechanisms of karate and those of power lifting and shot putting. A hint is the differences you see in the two distinctively varied kinds of *kiai* found in Jion. This would be a good subject to follow up on some day, but here we need to focus on *kiai* in *kumite*.

Our assumption is that, in order for us to have *kime*, our body muscles have to be tense. Isn't this what you learned in your training? I say this claim is correct but only partially. It is commonly believed that the whole body needs to be tense, like a bronze statue, in order to have *kime*. This is the very point I want to present as the biggest misconception that many practitioners and instructors seem to have. I felt so strongly about this belief on *kime* that I wrote what was originally an article for *Shotokan Karate Magazine* and is now included in this book as Chapter 1: "Kime."

By now, you have most likely already read the chapter, but the main point is that all the muscles of the body do *not* need to be tense in order to have *kime*. Better yet, they *must not* be tense if this *kime* is to be used in a real fight. What is needed is that only the selected muscles that are involved in generating and delivering power to the point of impact (i.e., the opponent) be tense. Regardless, in order to have *kime*, certain parts of the body, including the abdominal muscles and diaphragm, must be tense, and this is correct.

Well, then there must be *kiai* with *kime* as the tension must accompany the exhaling of the breath, right? No, this is exactly the point I take issue with. I wish for the reader to know that achieving *kime* while inhaling is not impossible. It is actually very possible if taught properly. In fact, one can train and learn to tense the diaphragm at three different phases of breathing: inhalation, exhalation, and holding. This means one can tense up at any time regardless of the breathing stage

Holding one's breath is commonly witnessed among beginners as they try to punch with full power. We all know that we exhale rapidly when we try to generate *kime* or *kiai*. Tensing the body while you inhale seems to be counterintuitive. When you inhale, you feel that your body naturally relaxes, and you are unable to tense. It does require a lot of training for one to learn to tense up the diaphragm while inhaling. This is one of the objectives in *ibuki* training—I talk about this later on in Chapter 11: "Hangetsu"—so it is not foreign to those *karateka* who are familiar with the breathing method.

Then, is it wrong to use *kiai* in *kumite*? My answer is twofold. If you are a *shodan* or *nidan*, I encourage you to have a loud *kiai* so you can learn to tense the inner muscles, including the diaphragms. Note that there are two of them. The diaphragm located underneath the lungs is well known, but most practitioners are unaware of or do not pay attention to the other one, which is located at the bottom of the stomach. If you are a higher-ranking practitioner, you need to learn how to have a soundless *kiai* in all your techniques.

Why should you have a soundless *kiai*? Well, if you are in a *kumite* tournament, this will not be an issue. But, if you are practicing karate as a martial art you must be prepared to face multiple opponents. This could mean not only two or three but possibly ten or even twenty of them. In this situation, your body movement must be highly energy effective. Your body tension must be extremely short, like one thousandth of a second (true *kime*), and this will result in a soundless *kiai* as even a short yell will not be possible. You may have a quick puff of air coming out of your slightly opened mouth, but that's it.

Along with such a breathing method, your physical movements will be extremely small or subtle to the point that your opponent may not even see you move. When your opponent steps forward to strike, you will simultaneously move in and engage him. You will pass by your opponent quietly as though nothing had happened between the two of you. But, the opponent will feel the impact a moment afterward, and that may put him down. This is a technique that Funakoshi tried to teach to his university students, but a period of four years was not long enough to reach this goal.

So, what is the bottom line for *kiai*? If you are a tournament competitor or are doing a fancy self-defense demonstration (photo below), go for it. Learn to let out a loud *kiai* so you can score your points. But, if you are a martial artist with, say, twenty years of training under your belt, you need to graduate from the loud *kiai*. Isn't it about time somebody starts teaching the art of the silent *kiai*?

Chapter Six
第六章

JKA Bunkai
日本空手協会による分解

I must confess that I have received quite a few criticisms and made many "enemies" because of this chapter since publishing the first edition of this book nearly ten years ago. I knew that this subject was controversial, but I did not expect some of the very negative criticism, which must have come from misunderstandings. For the third edition, I wish to add the following statement to clarify my stance on this subject.

Even though I stated this in the original edition, I would like to reemphasize that I was a faithful member of the JKA between 1963 and 2001. I learned almost all of the karate techniques I know from the JKA, and my karate foundation is definitely based on the JKA. I loved this organization, and I did not depart from it because of any dissatisfaction. I had no choice because the late Tetsuhiko Asai, former technical director of the JKA, left the JKA and founded his own organization, the JKS, in 2000. I wanted to follow Asai Sensei and learn Asai Ryu karate. This is why I had to resign from the JKA. In fact, leaving was a very difficult decision that took me a year to make. I still respect the JKA and its karate. I have many friends around the world, including Japan, who are still members of this organization.

Despite my deep respect and affection for this organization, I felt that I needed to expose the subject of JKA *bunkai*. As I had traveled around the world, I had met a huge number of practitioners, many of whom questioned the *bunkai* because they were not totally satisfied with its explanations. However, they were afraid to speak up about this, thinking they were not qualified to do so. So, they asked me, a Japanese instructor, to do this. Of course, I was unable to do so publicly while I was in the organization. But, after resigning, I figured it was about time to share regarding the problem concerning the *bunkai* explanations provided by JKA headquarters.

I believed then, and still do now, that the truth must be exposed for the sake of correct karate understanding, hoping it would benefit the reader. Before proceeding with this chapter, I would like to let the reader know that the reason I wrote this chapter was not to disrespect or dishonor the JKA but only to bring out the truth. I hope the reader will make his own decision as to whether or not my claim is legitimate after reading this chapter.

We all know that standard Shotokan karate training fundamentally consists of three parts: *kihon* (‘basics’), *kumite* (‘sparring’), and *kata* (‘forms’). Each part is supposedly equally important as a tool in achieving karate expertise. Unfortunately, out of these three, I find that *kata* is the most underestimated, misunderstood, and thus mismanaged aspect of karate training.

It is true that *kata* is a very unique tradition of Asian martial arts. Western martial arts, such as fencing, boxing, wrestling, and archery, did not develop this form of training. Indeed, *kata* is found in all Japanese martial arts, such as karate, kendo, judo (almost extinct but does exist), aikido, jujutsu, kyudo, iaido (居合道), *naginata* (薙刀), and many others. Moreover, the *kata* concept is so prevalent and important in Japanese culture that *kata* can be found in other Japanese arts and crafts, such as the tea ceremony known as *sado* (茶道) or *chanoyu* (茶の湯), the art of flower arrangement known as *kado* (華道) or *ikebana* (生け花), two types of classical Japanese dance known as *noh* (能) and *kabuki* (歌舞伎), the art of calligraphy known as *shodo* (書道), and even in cooking, carpentry, etc.

Let’s take a closer look at what karate *kata* is and what its purposes are so that we can understand why the ancient masters left it for us. If *kata* were, as is considered to be the case by some instructors, another form of *kihon*, it could not have survived over many hundreds of years.

Kata (形 or 型) is a Japanese word describing detailed patterns of specific movements (approximately twenty to one hundred) practiced either solo or as a team in which one steps and turns while attempting to maintain perfect form. The moves and the steps that are contained within the *kata* were determined by the ancient masters as the most fundamental and essential techniques chosen from numerous techniques they used in actual fighting. In karate *kata*, the practitioner is expected to visualize the enemy’s attacks and his own responses. *Karateka* “read” a *kata* in order to explain the imagined events.

There are perhaps more than 200 *kata* across the various styles of karate, each with many minor variations. Some *kata* are said to be handed down over several hundreds of years or more, and other *kata*, such as Heian, were created only a hundred years ago. ASAI (Asai Shotokan Association International) includes the *kata* Junro (順路) Shodan through Godan, which were created by Master Asai, in its standard syllabus. Other than those modern *kata*, the origins and history of *kata* are not clear as they were not well documented. However, the purpose of *kata* is very clear. *Kata* is a textbook of karate, and the following three functions (tools) are found in this textbook: a self-training tool, a combination-learning tool, and a knowledge-transferring tool.

Self-training Tool

Kata is a creative tool with which we can train all on our own. Even though karate skills are for use against an opponent, practicing alone has great value. Actually, it is better and more effective to train alone when you wish to perfect your techniques. This sounds contrary to what you may suppose, which is that you would perfect your techniques for real fighting situations during *kumite* practice. In actuality, most of the time, having an opponent is a deterrent to the process of perfecting your techniques. Why? Because you will be paying too much attention to your opponent's techniques—you do not want to get punched in the nose, of course. This means you are adjusting your techniques to match the opponent's.

To perfect your technique, you need to repeat the correct movements in the same manner hundreds or thousands of times. While doing a thousand punches or kicks is very boring and difficult to do on a daily basis, *kata* is perfect for carry ing out this monotonous process. You do not need to go to a dojo to practice *kata*. While you are on a business trip, a hotel room is big enough and you can turn it into your own dojo.

Combination-learning Tool

Kata is a long series of techniques, including many combinations, turns, jumps, etc., whereas *kihon* only takes out a segment (one technique or a short combination) in order to focus on improving that particular technique or short combination. By learning the form, or the fundamental moves, the practitioner can apply and modify the techniques to suit real situations that span numerous variations. A good analogy may be the process of learning a foreign language. We initially memorize a group of vocabulary words and then some basic sentences. This is like our *kihon*. Then, we study and memorize a series of question-and-answer exchanges, such as asking the way to the station, buying something, etc. This is our *kata*.

Western fighting arts such as wrestling, fencing, and boxing did develop some *kihon* moves, but these did not mature into *kata*. Interestingly, however, in classical music, students do some practice compositions that may be considered *kata*. The only difference is that there is no free sparring in classical music as you would find in jazz. A practice composition is done to prepare for much longer and more technically demanding compositions.

Knowledge-transferring Tool

At a time when people had no video or visual-aid equipment, a set of fixed movements (*kata*), which could be practiced repeatedly and handed down to other students, was a great tool for transferring the intricate technique exchanges. So, even though a master might pass away, his unique techniques would live on as long as his students practiced his *kata*, which contained said techniques. Although it is possible to write the techniques down on paper, it is extremely difficult to fully describe in written form all the finer points of the techniques that are contained in the long fighting sequences.

It is true that *kata* competition has become more popular in the tournaments of all the traditional karate styles. On the other hand, I hear that some instructors and practitioners have dropped *kata* training as they were not able to see the benefits to it or understand its relationship to *kumite*. This comes from ignorance of the applications (*bunkai* [分解]).

Another concern is that the tradition of *kata* has been changing lately and is possibly fading. A recent development in *kata* competition is that many competitors are modifying the rhythm and forms to make them look more dramatic for the purpose of getting higher scores in competitions. As a result, some of the *kata* no longer look like or have the precise techniques of the original *kata*. The third function of *kata*, knowledge transfer, is lost here.

In the process of my examination and study, I have found many misconceptions and misunderstandings that are associated with *kata* and its training. There are thousands of serious *karateka* who love *kata* and practice it diligently. Therefore, it is very unfortunate that these myths and misconceptions still exist and may continue to have some negative influence on them. In this chapter, I wish to expose these to the karate world and ask the reader if he agrees or disagrees. Regardless of which side the reader may be on, it is my hope that more people will have a better understanding of the true purpose of our *kata* and develop an appreciation for the heritage we were lucky to receive.

First of all, I want the reader to know that I had been a JKA member for over forty years when I switched to Asai Ryu karate in 2001. I did not leave the JKA on any ill terms, and I still have great respect for this organization. This chapter is certainly not intended to bash the JKA. My only intention is to expose a critical mistake it unfortunately made in the mid-1980s. It was a huge error that left—as I have witnessed—a huge impact on Shotokan karate training.

What I am talking about is a well-known official video produced by the JKA, titled *Original JKA Kata*

Series. I suspect many readers may own it or may have at least viewed it in the past. It is filmed with attractive backgrounds (temples, shrines, waterfalls, mountains, etc.) and performances by famous JKA instructors such as Nakayama, Osaka, Yahara, Imura, Tanaka, and many others. It was originally produced in VHS format and is now available in DVD format with English dubbing. One thing that is not known is that this film was created with overseas practitioners in mind. I will explain why this point is important later. David Hooper Sensei gives the following endorsement of this video:

> Not simply a way of learning Shotokan karate, but the ultimate reference against which one's progress should be measured. A professionally produced series of videotapes...that will serve as an infallible guide to the correct method of performing Shotokan *kata*.

I respect Hooper Sensei for his deep knowledge and many long years of training at the JKA headquarters in Japan. Actually, I have enjoyed reading many of his articles in *Shotokan Karate Magazine* and respect him greatly as a karate instructor. However, I just cannot accept that this video is "the ultimate reference" or "an infallible guide to the correct method of performing Shotokan *kata*." The demonstration of the *kata* is excellent, and this video definitely has value there. On the other hand, I have a serious issue with its *bunkai*. Frankly, many applications shown in this video are unrealistic and strange.

As you can see, those sensei apply the techniques and steps exactly the same way as they are required in the *kata*. You might ask, "So, what is the problem?" The problem is that they disregard or drop the true applications that are either hidden or modified movements in *kata*. In the video, those sensei perform so well that the techniques look natural and even realistic. I suspect most viewers believe all the *bunkai* techniques shown here are correct. Just try it yourself with the exact methods and steps shown in the video. You will find that many techniques do not work well. Do not blame your technique if you have problems as the *maai* and applications aren't realistic or applicable.

Here are some of the applications that I consider strange or unrealistic. I will also provide the applications I learned from Sugano Sensei and Asai Sensei. I would like to ask the reader to compare them to see which group of applications makes better or more realistic sense.

Heian Shodan (平安初段)

The very first two moves represent a block-and-counter combination. Unfortunately, this is the beginning of a series of unrealistic applications. Just think if you were the attacker. Would you step back after the first *chudan oi zuki* even if it were blocked? Most likely you would not. You would rather stay there and throw another attacking technique, such as a *gyaku zuki* or an *enpi uchi*, if the distance were short. If the attacker stays at the same position, the defender will not be able to step forward to throw an *oi zuki* as prescribed in Heian Shodan. It makes more sense for the defender to throw a *gyaku zuki* after a *gedan barai*. In the video, of course, the attacker conveniently steps back to allow for good *maai* for the defender, who can step forward to execute an *oi zuki*.

Why did the creator of Heian *kata*, Anko Itosu (Funakoshi's teacher), make the second move a step forward with a right *oi zuki*? There is a hidden technique in the very first move of Heian Shodan that is not mentioned or shown in the video. The first technique obviously looks like a left *gedan barai*, but it is more than just a block. It is actually a technique that includes another function, a *gedan* (or *chudan*) *kentsui uchi*. The defender steps in and blocks the attacker's *chudan zuki* with the elbow area rather than the wrist area and then continues to strike the attacker with a hammer fist. With this counterattack, the attacker may step back as seen in the *kata*, which would have been unnatural if the first move were only a block.

There is an additional hidden technique in the second move, called *ashi no kiri kaeshi* (足の切り返し, 'foot switchback'), which can be used in many other parts of the *kata*. For a fixed, short *maai*, you cannot take a full step forward, so instead you bring your left foot back to *heisoku dachi* and then take a quick step forward with your right foot to deliver a right *chudan oi zuki*. This footwork enables the defender to throw an *oi zuki* at a set distance.

Heian Nidan (平安二段)

The application of the first three moves (and that of the following three moves, which are performed as the mirror image) is a big problem. It is demonstrated in the video as a left *jodan uchi uke* with the right hand being just a *kamae* held over the forehead. Then, the second move is a very intricate punch-catching technique done by crossing the forearms. You see this kind of technique in kung fu movies, but would you teach this to eighth-*kyu* students?

The realistic application for the first move is as follows. You block a *jodan zuki* with your right *jodan age uke*—the right arm is not a *kamae*—while simultaneously striking the opponent's jaw with a left uppercut. This is a beautiful *morote* technique. The second move is a *chudan ura zuki* with your right fist while you pull your left fist back for the third movement (left *chudan zuki*).

Heian Sandan (平安三段)

Many would wonder about the second (left *gedan barai* and right *chudan uchi uke*) and third moves (right *gedan barai* and left *chudan uchi uke*). I am sure the reader will agree that the techniques demonstrated by the attacker in the video (a punch and a *mae geri* thrown as a simultaneous attack) are very unrealistic. I am not going to describe the details of the realistic *bunkai*, but it's an arm-twisting technique.

Heian Yondan (平安四段)

If the first move is a blocking technique, isn't it strange to turn to the other side to execute another block without applying any counterattacks after the first technique (or after the second technique)? In the JKA video, Osaka Sensei adds a knife-hand strike after the second movement, which is not in this *kata*. So, are there missing techniques? What is actually missing is the basic concept that the front hand is the attacking hand. The front knife hand is not a block but an attack. It is actually a thrust to the opponent's throat or a *teisho uchi* ('palm-heel strike') to his chin. The block is done by the rear hand in a similar way as what is seen in Nidan. With this application, the mystery of blocking-only techniques is solved.

Heian Godan (平安五段)

There is a jumping move after the *jodan ura zuki*. The video shows that this jump is to escape a *bo* strike to the knee area. The basic concept of this move is not strange; however, how do you explain the next move? Osaka Sensei uses this move (*gedan kosa uke*) with his legs crossed as his counter to the *bo* attacker. This application is very unnatural. The mystery is solved when we realize that most of the jumping techniques in *kata* are concealed throwing techniques. After the *jodan ura zuki*, you grab the opponent's *karategi* or clothes and throw him, using body rotation. If you have practiced judo, you can easily see how this is applied. When the throw is completed, you end up having your hands and feet in the positions shown. In *kata*, this movement is symbolized as a jump mainly to strengthen leg muscles and develop agility by means of the jumping movement.

There are many other strange and unrealistic applications throughout this video, but I do not think it is necessary to spend any more space in this chapter as the reader can easily find these by viewing the video with a more critical eye. I myself have not heard any comments expressing doubts or questions regarding these applications, though I have been in numerous Shotokan dojo. I wonder why no one has openly questioned or challenged this before.

Then, there is another big question. Why did the JKA produce this video in this way? Didn't Nakayama Sensei know the real applications? According to the late

Sugano Sensei (ninth *dan* and former vice chairman of the JKA) and Asai Sensei (technical director of the JKA at that time), who were also involved in the production of this video, Nakayama Sensei was seriously debating before production whether they would show the real *bunkai* or stick with the exact steps of the *kata*. He chose the latter for three major reasons.

The first reason was to show that all of the steps in Heian (Shodan through Godan) could be demonstrated and that *bunkai* could be applied in an as-is format. Though they had to force it, they needed to do this. Many non-Japanese practitioners visited the JKA *honbu* (本部) dojo in the sixties and seventies and asked for *bunkai* in order to better understand *kata*. This is a very natural thing for Westerners, but this kind of inquiry is very rare for Japanese students. The JKA had to show or prove that all the moves in Heian *kata* would work in *bunkai* in order to satisfy the non-Japanese students. Those sensei performed so well in the video that no one who viewed it felt that the applications were unnatural or unrealistic.

Another reason for the JKA applications came from the concept that all *kata* start and end with a block. To prove this, they had to use the front arm for the blocking techniques. Actually, this is a misconception itself. In fact, the forward fist is designed as an attacking technique in almost all *kata*. It is a shame, but it is true that this correct concept is completely ignored in the JKA video. In the following chapter, I discuss in depth this misconception that all *kata* start and end with an *uke* in order to reveal where this idea came from and why they had to honor it.

The final reason is even more controversial. It was also true that Nakayama Sensei and the other JKA sensei did not want to show the true *bunkai* to the public, particularly to Westerners. It was not much of a problem to hide these things in

Japan as the students do not ask questions there. If a certain *kata* is taught, then the students diligently practice it thousands of times without any doubts or questions.

However, as I mentioned above, in the sixties and seventies, more and more Westerners picked up karate and started to ask questions about the applications. The instructors were hesitant to show the true applications, which require the modification of moves and a lot of complex explanations. They were not good at making long and complex explanations as that is an uncommon practice in Japan, particularly in a martial arts situation. Besides, the JKA sensei feared that, by knowing the true applications, the overseas students would mistakenly consider the *kata* moves to be incorrect and would change the *kata* moves to fit the applications.

As a result, they failed to explain to the students that *kata* represents only the textbook movements. In fact, there isn't one absolutely correct application for each movement. Actually, there are many variations and different interpretations. *Kata* represents the most common and effective movements along with many hidden ideas and techniques. This would take a lot of explanation and a much longer video, and this is why Nakayama Sensei opted to produce a simple and straightforward video showing one *bunkai* method in order to avoid possible confusion in the relationship of *kata* to *bunkai.*

This was tremendously unfortunate and also ironic. I feel that this beautifully produced film has resulted in more harm than good regarding non-Japanese practitioners' true understanding of *kata* as it relates to its *bunkai.*

Chapter Seven
第七章

Begin and End with Blocks
形は受けで始まり受けで終わるのか

A popular and incorrect belief regarding our *kata* is that all of them begin and end with a blocking technique. I was told by my sensei, the late Jun Sugano (菅野淳, 1928–2002), that some *kata* may start with an *uke waza* (受け技, 'blocking technique') but that the last move is never a block. Note that, in some cases, the last move may look like an *uke*, but it is actually a *zanshin* (残心) movement. Some examples are discussed below.

In the previous chapter, I already pointed out that the first moves of Heian Shodan, Nidan, and Yondan are not blocks. Now let us look at some of the main Shotokan *kata* and examine their first and last moves to illustrate this important point. The *bunkai* described below are based on the teaching I received from Sugano Sensei. I understand that there are many interpretations to these *kata*. One is to follow the application based on the literal names of the movements; thus, the first and last moves can always be blocks. I request that the reader evaluate the *bunkai* presented here and compare them to the *bunkai* that begin and end with blocks. I would like to challenge the reader to see which interpretation makes more sense and is more realistic.

Bassai Dai (抜塞大)

The first move is called *morote chudan uke*. The technique for this move is a combination of a left *osae uke* ('pressing block') and a simultaneous right *uraken uchikomi*. This very first move symbolizes the *kata* Bassai, which means 'taking out a fortress'. Sugano Sensei used to tell us, "Strike to break open a heavy door with this move." This *kata* must start with a devastating striking or attacking technique. If one starts this *kata* with the feeling of doing a block first, he will miss out on the true character of Bassai *kata*.

The final move is a *shuto uke*, but it is easier to interpret it as an attack. We do this move with a *kiai*, and it is definitely done as a knife-hand strike, not as a block.

Kanku Dai (観空大)

Although the first move, where the open hands go up above the head and then return to the bottom in a circular motion, can be interpreted as an arm-locking motion against two opponents holding the shoulders, this move is commonly interpreted as being simply a ritual bowing motion. The movement from the top in a large outward circle signifies a preparedness to fight and/or an opening of one's spirit to the fight. Sugano Sensei used to say, "Now you are opening the gate of your castle." It is comparable to the very last move, where the arms initially make an outward circle and then turn into an inward circle as they descend and finally rest at *yoi* position. This motion signifies the closing of one's castle gate with a *zanshin* feeling.

So, with the interpretation that the first and last movements are ritualistic, the first actual fighting moves are the *jodan shuto* techniques, which are similar to the first techniques of Heian Yondan. This movement, a quick motion in Kanku, is named *shuto uke* but is actually a disguised *nukite* or *shuto uchi*. If the first two techniques were two blocks to the left and right sides, it really would not make sense. We would have to ask what happens to the opponent after the *jodan shuto uke*. Does he get scared and run away? Does he move to the other side and attack again? Interpreting these two quick *shuto* moves as a fast *jodan* strike to each side (striking two opponents who have stepped in to punch from either side of the defender) is more natural and makes more sense.

The last fighting move (the one before the ritualistic large circular movement of the arms as described above) is a *nidan geri* followed by a *jodan uraken uchikomi*. It is done with a *kiai*, and no one will disagree that this is an attacking movement.

Hangetsu (半月)

The first move is indeed a *chudan uchi ude uke*, a blocking technique. The main purpose of this *kata* is to learn *hangetsu dachi*, and the creator of the *kata* chose *uchi ude uke* as the first movement. This first move could also have been a *gedan barai* as it requires similar body tension, but the creator picked *uchi ude uke*. Hangetsu is unique in that it came from Naha Te (那覇手), whereas most Shotokan *kata* are from Shuri Te. Hangetsu is truly distinctive as a Shotokan *kata* as it is the only *kata* expected to be performed with heavy breathing exercises as seen in many Goju Ryu *kata*, such as Sanchin and Tensho.

Now you might say, "The last move, *gedan morote teisho uke*, is definitely a blocking technique." Yes, it does look like it, but, if you investigate the history and development of this *kata*, you will find that this move is a modification of a *shuto mawashi uke* with a simultaneous *jodan teisho uchi*. Compare the preparatory moves of this particular technique (one hand pulled near the chest and the other pulled to the hip) to those of Hangetsu (both *shuto* pulled back to the hips). You will realize that they are very similar, and you will see the connection between these techniques. Nevertheless, some practitioners also consider the *morote teisho uke* to be a *zanshin* move following a *kime* with the *gedan gyaku zuki*. However, am sure the reader will agree that the first interpretation is more natural and believable.

Gankaku (岩鶴)

Indeed, the very first move of this *kata* looks like a blocking technique. However, if you think about this peculiar (or unnatural) hand movement, you will be able to understand that there is a hidden technique here. It is, in fact, a *jodan morote shuto hasami uchi* but modified to look like a block. This combination of *jodan juji uke* (or *shuto hasami uchi*), *morote osae uke*, and *nihon zuki* was incorporated into Heian Godan.

The last move, the *oi zuki* after the *yoko geri*, does not need to be explained or debated.

Enpi (燕飛)

The first move is a hard one to interpret. You lightly kneel down as you block downward with your right fist and bring your left fist across your chest. What does this mean? This is actually a *tsukami uke*, which is for grabbing the opponent with your right hand while simultaneously executing a left *kagi zuki*. Again, this is a hidden technique that needs to be explained by an instructor who understands the real application of this *kata*.

Toward the end of the *kata*, there is a jump, which also has a hidden application. As explained in Heian Godan, the jump in Enpi is a throwing technique, as well. The right *kokutsu shuto uchi* is the real last movement, in which a strike is directed at the opponent who has just been thrown down. The next move, which is a step back into a left *kokutsu dachi* with a *shuto uke*, is not a blocking technique but rather a *zanshin* movement performed as you step away from the fallen opponent.

Jion (慈恩)

The first move is similar to that of Heian Sandan. The *bunkai* in the JKA video shows this as a double block against an opponent who attacks with a double punch or a simultaneous punch and kick. It is better to interpret this move as an arm-twisting technique directed at an opponent who grabs your shoulders. It is also commonly considered to be a *kamae* position before a fight.

The last move is obviously a right *chudan zuki*, which is an attack.

Jutte (十手)

This *kata* was created based on the concept of fighting against opponents with staffs. It is difficult to interpret the applications nowadays as this *kata* is not taught in that context anymore. It has been changed so that the techniques can be used against empty-handed opponents.

The first move is a *maki otoshi uke* ('wrist-twisting dropping block'), and it is indeed blocking an opponent's staff in order to grab it and take it away.

The last moves are a series of *jodan age uke*, but they are actually not *age uke* when you are fighting an opponent with a staff. The fists are closed, but they hold a staff, and the real position of the fists is similar to what you will find in Meikyo (one fist near your forehead and the other in front at *gedan*). This supposed sequence of *age uke* techniques is actually a disguised leg-sweeping and throwing technique using a staff.

There are many other well-known *kata*, but I believe I have picked a sufficient number of samples here to make my point. After reviewing all these *kata*, we must ask why the Shotokan masters, including Funakoshi Sensei, agreed to the statement "All *kata* begin and end with blocking techniques." As far as I know, there are at least three different reasons or causes for this myth.

Reason 1

In order to understand the first reason, we have to look at the history of Shotokan. In the early twentieth century, Funakoshi Sensei had to propagate karate in Japan. He was poor and unknown. He needed a sponsor in Japan to be successful, and that person was Jigoro Kano (嘉納治五郎, 1860–1938 [photo right]), the founder of judo.

After observing a demonstration by Funakoshi Sensei, Kano Sensei was very impressed by his karate techniques. He actually proposed that Funakoshi Sensei affiliate himself with Kodokan Judo (講道館柔道) and that he be a part of the organization. Funakoshi Sensei diplomatically declined the offer, but he had to work closely with Kano Sensei, who was extremely influential in the fields of education and athletics in Japan. Because he was fluent in English, Kano Sensei was an official Olympic committee representative sent to meetings in Europe in the early twentieth century.

As most readers know, judo came from jujutsu. Kano Sensei removed some of the more blatantly dangerous techniques from jujutsu in order to make judo safer and more attractive to the public. Most of the techniques that Kano Sensei left out were the hitting and kicking techniques that had come from hand-to-hand combat during the feudal era of the thirteenth and fourteenth centuries. Funakoshi Sensei did not want to portray karate as a threat to judo. So, he presented Kano Sensei with the concept that all *kata* began and ended with blocking techniques; thus, karate was a very "defensive" martial art.

Reason 2

After World War II, the occupation army prohibited the Japanese from practicing any martial arts. They considered the samurai spirit to be the reason that the Japanese military had fought so ferociously. (The kamikaze pilots never gave up but rather committed *harakiri*, carried out banzai attacks, etc.) They thought that martial arts training would encourage hostility toward the occupation army.

However, in the late forties, Funakoshi Sensei and some other karate masters approached GHQ and asked for karate training to be permitted. They repeated this same statement, that karate was a very defensive martial art, and their proof was that all *kata* began and ended with blocking techniques.

Reason 3

There is another reason that some of the present-day Japanese sensei continue to publicly repeat this same myth. The following reason can be controversial, and some Japanese instructors may strongly disagree with it, but the statement "All *kata* begin and end with blocking techniques" is often used because, unfortunately, karate has a bad or poor image in Japan.

When karate was first introduced into Japan from Okinawa nearly a hundred years ago, the Japanese public knew nothing of this art. Karate was perceived as an overtly dangerous skill. It met with a similar perception in the U.S. right after World War II, when the G.I.s brought it home. Some practitioners (particularly poor ones) used this wrong image to make themselves appear more powerful or intimidating. They frequently bragged about their skills and helped spread this wrong image in the early days of karate development.

Before World War II, there was a popular movie called *Sugata Sanshiro* (姿三四郎 [Toho Studios, 1943]), in which the eponymous character is a judo expert who has a duel with a scruffy and unhealthy-looking karate guy. The karate guy uses "unfair" techniques and "cheats" (to emphasize his bad character), but, in the end, the judo guy wins. It was a typical good-guy-versus-bad-guy movie, but it certainly gave karate a bad name.

In the eighties and nineties, full-contact karate tournaments became very popular in Japan. The public saw many bashed fists and bloody faces on TV. These images certainly gave the public a bad impression of karate, although some young people thought it was cool. In addition, there were a few unfortunate accidental deaths in some university karate clubs. Although these accidents were infrequent, people wrongly got a sense that karate was an overtly dangerous martial art.

With all these misconceptions of karate, you cannot blame those sensei for emphasizing the self-defense part of karate and impressing upon the public its nonaggressive aspects.

Regardless of the reasons, it is a hidden fact that the *kata* we practice do not necessarily start and never end with an *uke waza*. I hope that, by knowing this, our mental attitude at the beginning and end of the *kata* will be different from when we thought those techniques were only blocks.

Chapter Eight
第八章

Return to Starting Point
形は開始所定地に戻る

When we do *kata*, is it really mandatory that we come back to the exact spot where we started? I can almost hear your reply: "Yes, Nakayama Sensei said so in *Best Karate*." You are absolutely correct. He listed these six important points for *kata* in that famous book:

1. Correct order
2. Beginning and end
3. Meaning of each movement
4. Awareness of target
5. Rhythm and timing
6. Proper breathing

For Item 2 above, he clearly stated, "*Kata* must begin and end at the same spot on the *enbusen*. This requires practice." If you are in a tournament, this is absolutely a requirement, isn't it? The photo on the right shows a typical tournament floor with the starting/ending point visibly marked. If you are off by, say, three feet, I am sure those careful judges will take some points off of your performance.

Have you ever wondered why there is such a requirement? Nakayama Sensei did not explain why in his book. Maybe it is just a natural thing, and you may think I am wasting my time by asking this. But, I have wondered about this and foolishly investigated it for many years. I was curious to know if the creators of *kata* (for example, Itosu and his Heian *kata*) really designed all *kata* in such a way that the performer would always return to the starting point.

After much investigation and direct questioning, I have concluded that this is not the case. Someone changed the rule and created this new requirement of coming back to the exact starting point. I wanted to find out who was behind this and what the reasons for it were. This is a mystery, and I wish to share my findings and my theory on this mystery with you here.

If you are a *nidan* or above, you must have learned Chinte (珍手), and this *kata* could be your tournament *kata*, especially if you are a female practitioner. We know this is a very unique *kata*—*chinte* literally means 'unique hand' or 'strange hand'—but do you realize it also has a very unique (strange) ending (three hops backward)? I have researched for many years and asked many sensei about these ending steps. For the longest time, no one could give me a believable *bunkai* for these unique moves with the feet in *heisoku dachi* and the hands clasped together. It had been a big mystery to me, as I could not figure out the meaning of these strange hops.

The following is what I have found in the process of investigation. One Japanese sensei, whose name I cannot reveal, told me it was for balance training. Yes, it is indeed difficult to keep balance with your feet and hands pressed together. But, if you think it through, it just does not make any sense as you still wonder why they were put at the end of the *kata*. After the final delivery of a *kime* technique (here the right *gyaku zuki* to *chudan* with a *kiai*), we can expect a *zanshin* move as seen with the last step in Enpi. However, why would anyone use three unstable backward-hopping steps as a *zanshin* move? Even if you buy into the idea of having this balancing move here, why hop with both feet together? Hopping on just one foot would be more of a martial arts move (like the *tsuru ashi dachi* in Gankaku). No matter how much I have considered the possibility, I cannot buy into this theory.

Another sensei, an American, told me that it was a case of escaping backward with your hands and feet tied together. Hmm, interesting. But, in all honesty, when I heard this, I almost burst out laughing. I could barely contain myself, but I did not want to be rude to him as he was deadly serious. I followed up with a natural question: "Why or how would one get his hands and feet tied together at that moment in the *kata*?" Unfortunately, he did not have an answer to that question.

One other explanation was that this move is a pulling and takedown technique. I believe this was demonstrated by one of the Japanese JKA instructors in Europe. After punching your own left hand (representing an imaginary target) with your right fist, you grab the opponent with both hands and pull him toward you. Then, you continue to pull the opponent while taking three steps to take him down.

The person from whom I got this information said that the demonstration was very convincing. Yes, that application is doable and may be reasonable. But, my question regarding this explanation was this: "Why is it done while hopping with the feet together?" Yes, I am aware that some *kata* moves are disguised. A good example is the jump in Enpi and the one in Heian Godan. It is not a jump over a striking staff aimed at your lower legs, as is commonly believed, but rather a throwing technique. However, how do you explain the reason for the three hops? Remember that the technique right before those hops is a *gyaku zuki* with *kime* (symbolized by a *kiai*), which means that this technique should drop the opponent. Then, why would a fighter drag his opponent three times if he is already down? Even with such a convincing demonstration, this cannot fully explain the idea behind these hops.

And finally, Gennosuke Higaki (桧垣源之助), another Japanese sensei and the author of the famous book *Hidden Karate* (隠されていた空手 [Champ, 2006]), responded to my inquiry. He explained that those steps were added to put the performer back at the original starting spot. When I read his letter, I said to myself, *Yes, this must be the right answer*. Even though I do not rely on information from *Wikipedia*, I will make an exception again as I think the statement I found under its entry on Chinte is interesting:

> Some believe the final three movements, a series of backwards hops, were added to bring the *kata* back to the original starting place in order to facilitate competition, because they are not present in the other versions of the *kata* practiced by other styles of Japanese karate.

To verify this, I checked a few other styles for this *kata*, namely, Shito Ryu and Okinawa Kyudokan (沖縄究道館). In Shito Ryu, the name of the *kata* is read as either *Chinte* or *Chintei*, and sometimes it is also called *Shoin* (松陰). In Kyudokan, it is read as *Chinti*. These *kata* indeed do not have the three hops at the end. If you are interested in watching these *kata*, you can find video clips on *YouTube*.

I would like to share an old memory of mine relating to this subject. This happened back in the late seventies. My old karate friend Sal Lopresti Sr.—he is now seventh *dan* and the chief instructor of Shotokan Karate Jutsu International in New Jersey (www.shotokankaratejutsu.com/home.html)—performed Chinte in the final round of the ISKF/JKA-hosted East Coast Championships. I remember this incident clearly because I was strongly disturbed. I witnessed a point deduction for his having done four hops instead of three. Of course, at that time, I did not know the true meaning of these hops, but I still thought it was unfair to lose a point just for doing an extra hop. His *kata* performance was excellent, but Sal missed placing first because of this "mistake." I communicated with him recently about this incident, and he told me that he certainly remembered it very well, and with some bitter feelings.

In the previous chapter, I wrote about several *kata*, including Bassai Dai, Kanku Dai, Gankaku, Enpi, etc., but I excluded Chinte because of this particular ending. I did so intentionally as I wanted to discuss this controversial subject in a separate chapter, this one.

OK, I have said enough about Chinte. We can look at another case, the Heian *kata* that we all take for granted. By reviewing the Okinawan Pin'an Nidan (Shotokan's Heian Shodan), I discovered that there had been a change in the last four steps of Heian Shodan, i.e., the *kokutsu dachi* and *shuto uke* techniques.

From the last *chudan oi zuki* (with *kiai*), you turn 270 degrees in a counter-clockwise direction, pivoting on your right foot. You end up in a left *kokutsu dachi* with a *shuto uke*. The angle of this rotation is the key point. In the Okinawan *kata*, you rotate only 225 degrees.

For the next step, the Shotokan *kata* has a step through with the right foot into a right *kokutsu dachi* at about the 10:30 spot with a *shuto uke*. However, the Okinawan *kata* just has a step straight forward.

As we know, the second-to-last step in the Shotokan *kata* is a 135-degree clockwise rotation. This is a 90-degree clockwise rotation in the Okinawan *kata*. The very last step in the Shotokan *kata* is a step through with the left foot into a left *kokutsu dachi* at about the 1:30 spot, but it is another straight move forward in the Okinawan *kata*.

Pinan Nidan Kata

NOTE: This shows the basic pattern and is NOT drawn to scale.
The drawing is only to give an idea of the general directions in which the body moves.
The dot represents the starting point as you face the top of the drawing.

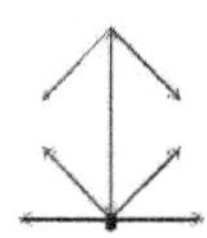

It is obvious that the original steps found in the Okinawan *kata* will result in a different ending place. With the Okinawan *kata* you can easily guess that you will end up one or two steps in front of the starting point. Take a look at this video of Okinawan Shorin Ryu's Pin'an Nidan: www.youtube.com/watch?v=KbRjp5Ahc04.

All serious Shotokan karate practitioners must see how Heian, the fundamental and core Shotokan *kata*, was performed in the original way. We see clear differences in the stances but more distinctly in the way the hips are used. This is called *muchimi* (餅身), which literally means 'rice-cake body'. As this is not the subject of this chapter, I will not delve into this unique character of Okinawan karate which has been lost in modern-day Shotokan karate.

There is no record of who made the changes to these last four steps or when they were made. The same changes were also made to the last four steps of Heian Nidan (i.e., the sequence of *zenkutsu dachi gedan barai* and *jodan age uke*). Heian Sandan, Yondan, and Godan do not share the same issue because of their origina movement patterns.

This is indeed a mystery. But, there is another mystery with Heian Shodan. As you may know, the original Heian Shodan was called *Heian Nidan* and vice versa. Therefore, someone switched these two *kata* around. It is not well known or documented who switched Shodan and Nidan. But, obviously, the original Heian Shodan (our Nidan) was too difficult for beginners. I plan to reveal my theory at the end of this chapter. Regardless of who changed these four steps and the order of Shodan and Nidan, I can surely say that the person did it with the definite intention of correcting something.

Let's check into how Heian Shodan is done by Shotokai practitioners. Here is the URL: www.youtube.com/watch?v=RHz0hPUxeS0.

This video was made sometime in the early seventies. As you can see in the video, the pattern of the steps of Heian Shodan is identical to that of the JKA. The founder of the Shotokai, Shigeru Egami, started karate under Funakoshi in 1933 at Waseda University. The Shotokai is known for strictly adhering to Funakoshi's teaching, and Egami would not have dreamed of changing Funakoshi's *kata*. So, I assume Heian Shodan has been practiced in that stepping pattern since at least the early thirties.

In the centuries before the twentieth, the art of karate was taught only on a one-to-one basis on Okinawa. In other words, a sensei had only one or two students at any given time. A good example of this is Funakoshi's case, where he was the only student of Anko Azato (安里安恒, 1827–1906). When you consider the one-to-one teaching environment, it becomes evident that a student would be corrected immediately if he missed any steps. I am sure the teacher would pay more attention to the student's rhythm, timing, speed, power, and holistic body movement than to whether or not he was coming back to the starting point. The priority level of where a student's *kata* ended would have been very low in a one-teacher-to-one-student environment.

On Okinawa, large-class training started only at the turn of the twentieth century, after karate had become one of the PE courses in high school (1901). Itosu was behind the introduction of karate into the public schools on Okinawa, and he must have created the Heian *kata* series in the late nineteenth century for such education. Heian *kata* was adopted for teaching large PE classes in 1904.

Okinawan high school PE students participate in mass Heian *kata* training in this historic picture taken in front of Shuri Castle in the early 1900s.

It is also worthwhile to study further by reviewing how Shito Ryu practitioners perform Pin'an (Heian) *kata*. Here is a video of Pin'an Nidan (our Heian Shodan): www.youtube.com/watch?v=vE0lAyVMkDI.

Shito Ryu is a sister style of Shotokan (sharing the Itosu lineage as a root). The founder of this style was Kenwa Mabuni (摩文仁賢和, 1889–1952), who learned Shuri Te from Itosu and Naha Te from Kanryo Higaonna (東恩納寛量, 1853–1915). Higaonna was sensei to Chojun Miyagi, the founder of Goju Ryu. After moving to mainland Japan in 1929, Mabuni founded Shito Ryu in Osaka in 1934.

Shotokan and Shito Ryu share many *kata* under the same names. However, the movements are performed quite differently. It is an interesting subject to compare the differences of technique execution between the two styles, particularly on the stances, arm movements, and kicks.

What is interesting about Shito Ryu's Pin'an Nidan (our Heian Shodan) is that they did not change the directions of the last four movements but rather kept them the original way. Instead, they changed the directions of the four moves after the first *kiai* (i.e., the sequence of four *kokutsu dachi shuto uke*). By doing this, the performer will end up one step closer to the starting point, which, as a result, cancels out the one step in the opposite direction resulting from the very last four moves.

They have essentially done the same thing as what modern-day Shotokan has done, that is, modify this basic *kata* from the original Okinawan method so that the performer returns to the starting point. I assume Mabuni implemented this change after he moved to Japan. My guess is that Funakoshi, having moved to Japan several years ahead of Mabuni, told him about his idea, which had been very helpful in teaching Japanese students. Moreover, having a starting spot also worked well once they started *kata* competitions.

You will find another interesting factor when you look at *kata* from wushu or kung fu. Even though I am not an expert in the study of Chinese styles, from the several dozens I have seen, some of these *kata* do not end in the same spot where they started. In some cases, the performer ends up very far away from the starting point and sometimes even facing different directions. Since the ancient Okinawan *karateka* learned *kata* from kung fu teachers, this concept of what we are discussing could not have come from kung fu influences.

After evaluating all of the factors I have mentioned above, I conclude that the ancient creators of Okinawan *kata* would not have considered it critical or necessary for the practitioner to return to the exact starting point of the *kata*.

So, who was the person responsible for this key change from the original Heian *kata* movements to the current patterns? Could it have been Itosu as he was the one who created Heian for public education? We can deduce that Itosu did not switch Shodan and Nidan. I can say this because Shito Ryu kept the original order of Shodan and Nidan. If Itosu had switched the names, then his disciple Mabuni, the founder of Shito Ryu, would have done the same just as Shotokan had done.

Then, how about the last four steps of Heian Shodan and Nidan? Did Itosu change these steps to make a better fit for mass teaching? If Itosu were the person who changed the steps, then Okinawan Shorin Ryu would have the same steps. But, it does not. And, it is hardly believable to think that Itosu told only Funakoshi to make those changes.

By now, I guess the reader will have already guessed who it was. With all the factors pointing to him and the fact that he was a born educator (a career high school teacher until he moved to Tokyo), Funakoshi had to be the person who came up with and enacted these changes with the belief that they would help Japanese students, particularly in self-training. I believe it was originally done for educational (teaching methodology) purposes only. Obviously, Shodan is a much simpler *kata* than Nidan, which has many advanced techniques, including a kick.

So, why did Itosu set Heian Nidan as the first *kata*? This is also a small mystery, but this is what I think. If you examine Heian Nidan very closely, you will realize its close similarity to Kanku Dai. Itosu must have thought that the simplified version of Kanku Dai should be the first *kata* for public education. This idea is understandable from a martial artist's perspective, but Funakoshi, as a former high school teacher, believed that Heian Shodan was much easier for high school and college students to learn as the first *kata*. Therefore, he reversed these two *kata*.

As a side note, I came across a book recently that would substantiate my hypothesis. The book is called *Karate: Pin'an Katas in Depth* (Empire Books, 2006) and was written by Keiji Tomiyama, who resides in the UK. In his introduction (pages 1–4), Tomiyama states, "Because of this fact, it is the general practice to teach beginners Nidan first before Shodan. Master Gichin Funakoshi, founder of the Shotokan style of karate, actually swapped the positions of these *kata* and renamed them." Tomiyama is a Shito Ryu stylist, so I do not know how he came to know the historical actions of Funakoshi, but I was happy to find this statement.

How about the last four steps of Shodan and Nidan? As I have described before, these changes were implemented for beginners so that they could check themselves to see if they had done the steps correctly. If a student did not miss any steps, and all the steps were executed with uniform length and in the right directions, he would come back to the same spot where he had started.

Then, who else could come up with such a smart change? Nobody else but Funakoshi. Here is a very interesting and revealing paragraph from *Karate Do Kyohan* (from the section "Line of Movement" on page 41). The paragraph is a bit long, but I would like to quote it here:

> "Whatever goes must come back": in karate, the points at which one starts and completes the *kata* must coincide, and failure in this indicates either that an incorrect step has been taken or that variation in lengths of stride has caused deviation from the correct positions. Since karate depends in a very real way on the stability of the hips and not just on the use of the arms, length of stride and positions of the feet must be practiced with particular thoroughness. Whatever goes will return: it is in order to facilitate the assimilation of this rule that in each figure referring to the *kata* the position of the corresponding steps is indicated relative to the line of movement, and one must adhere strictly to these diagrams in practice.

I do not know if he anticipated or even dreamed that this concept of starting and ending at the same spot would become a mantra that would haunt not only Shotokan but all traditional karate styles after his death.

Interestingly, the first JKA national championship tournament was held in 1957, the year Funakoshi passed away. This requirement was strictly enforced after competition became popular in the sixties and seventies. So, you can deduct a point if a competitor hops four times in Chinte.

If you are highly motivated to win in a tournament, then there is nothing wrong with focusing on returning to the starting spot. However, if you are a martial artist—and I hope many readers are—your desire must be to do the *kata* for what they were originally created for: practicing fighting techniques. Then, you will agree that we must pay more attention to the really important aspects of *kata*, such as stable stances, smooth body shifting, balance, imaginary opponents, the effective applications of the techniques, power, rhythm, timing, and so on.

Both the final technique and the recovery at the end of the *kata* are extremely important. You have delivered the final blow and survived the battle. At that moment, you want to maintain that *zanshin* feeling, where you must have a clear and alert mind plus normal and controlled breathing until you do the final *rei* (礼, 'bow'). While you are going through this process at that critical moment of fighting, how important is it to think or worry about the spot where you put your last step? Wouldn't it possibly be the last thing on your mind?

If you are interested in seeing more about Shorin Ryu karate, an all-Japanese video with English subtitles can be found here: www.youtube.com/watch?v=CfND0Nwrc3E.

If you are interested in seeing other topics on Okinawan karate, here is a video in English: www.youtube.com/watch?v=F15m9R2Zi2o.

Chapter Nine
第九章

Mystery Kata Tekki Shodan Part I
鉄騎初段の不思議　パート１

When you think of Tekki, you probably think of two unique characteristics: the *kiba dachi* and the sideways-only movement. Many readers might have wondered about the reasons for the uniqueness of this *kata*. You may also find it difficult to figure out how to turn the techniques of this *kata* into applications. Besides that, you move like a crab, and you may consider this to be a boring *kata*.

Let me tell you that I have been practicing Shotokan karate for over fifty years and have found Tekki to be an extremely valuable and useful *kata* among those I have learned so far, including the twenty-six JKA *kata* and an additional twenty-six Asai *kata*. It is true that this is the only JKA *kata* with an *enbusen* (演武線) that is lateral, but there are two more *kata* outside the JKA that have a lateral *enbusen*. They are called *Kibaken* and *Tekki Mugen*, and they were created by Asai Sensei.

Back to Tekki, the *enbusen* is definitely not the only unique aspect of this *kata*; there are many more. As you read this chapter, I hope you will discover the hidden wisdom and unparalleled ingenuity of the creator who designed this *kata*. I have tremendous respect for the creator and am amazed by his ingenuity.

When you start karate lessons, your first *kata* is Heian Shodan. Some dojo may teach Taikyoku (太極) *kata* before Heian, but Taikyoku is a simplified version of Heian, so I consider them to be in the same group. When you pass your fifth-*kyu* test with Heian Godan, you are promoted to fourth *kyu*, one step before brown belt. At this time, you learn Tekki Shodan, a very different *kata* from all of the Heian *kata*. Many fourth-*kyu* students are perplexed and ask the instructor what this *kata* is all about. I am afraid not too many instructors are equipped to give them the full and comprehensive explanation that I believe students deserve to receive.

Anyway, after you pass the third-*kyu* exam and become a brown belt, I suspect that you basically forget about Tekki. Am I correct? You are under the impression that you need to move on to a "real" *kata*, Bassai Dai, which is more difficult and must be more important. I can hear you saying, "I spent three months practicing Tekki when I was a fourth *kyu*. Now I am a *shodan*"—or *nidan* or whatever rank you may be—"and my teacher does not expect me to practice Tekki anymore. Besides, I never see anyone doing this *kata* in any of the tournaments."

What you are stating is true, but I am not saying that the current trend is good or favorable. I am just saying that it is the common trend and that many students are under the impression that Tekki *kata* is not important. Indeed, I only practiced Tekki Shodan for three months to take my third-*kyu* test but practiced Bassai Dai for over a year before my *shodan* exam.

After studying the history of Okinawan karate, I found that students practiced Tekki for more than three years as they did not have Heian *kata* before Itosu invented it in the late nineteenth century, a little over a hundred years ago. By introducing Heian *kata*, the length of Tekki Shodan was significantly reduced. In addition, when Funakoshi introduced karate into Japan, the importance of this *kata* and the teaching of it were not emphasized as much as they had been on Okinawa. So, we wonder why. Later in this chapter, I will attempt to introduce some insight as to why Tekki *kata* lost its rightful position of importance in Shotokan.

This *kata* was originally called *Naihanchi* (ナイハンチ or 内歩進). (Note that there are many other similar-sounding names on Okinawa, such as *Naihanching*, *Naifanchi*, etc.) Funakoshi changed the Okinawan names of the *kata* to more Japanese-like names, and he chose *Tekki* for this one. *Tekki* (鉄騎) literally means 'iron horse riding', and the reason he chose this name is obvious as he must have wanted practitioners to train their legs to build a strong and steady stance.

As far as the original name of this *kata* (*Naihanchi*) is concerned, the meaning changes depending on the Chinese characters you apply to it. The origin of this *kata* is obscure; thus, even the Okinawan name is most likely not the true name of the original. One thing is clear, however, and that is that *nai* (内) means 'internal' or 'inside'. Tekki *kata* does employ many short-distance fighting techniques, so *nai* must imply these techniques.

In addition, I believe there are more interpretations for *nai*. It actually has at least two more points. One is the leg-moving method using the inside thigh muscles. It is a shame that the modern-day *kiba dachi* has lost its inside tension as it is now described as an outward stance. The same change can be witnessed in Hangetsu *kata*, which I explain in Chapter 11: "Hangetsu." The very first movement from *heisoku dachi* to *kosa dachi* is a good example of a leg-shifting move using the inside thigh muscles.

The other meaning of *nai* is a reference to the tension and relaxation of the upper-body muscles. The details of this will be described in the latter part of this chapter, so let me give just a summary here. In the very fixed stance of *kiba dachi*, you are required to deliver the techniques to the left and right. It is not too challenging to deliver a technique to the left side with your left arm or to the right side with your right arm. What makes it challenging, which I suspect you have found in your performance, is trying to deliver a full technique to the left side with your right arm, which requires your upper body to rotate at least ninety degrees (see the photo of Funakoshi below).

The shoulder line will cross the line between the feet at a right angle. Keeping a perfect *kiba dachi* during the rotation is quite difficult, so most people have an imperfect *kiba dachi* with one knee (typically on the reverse side) bent in. Perfect movements require trained flexibility of the midsection and control of the internal muscles and organs.

Hidden Karate, which is one of the books I referred to in the previous chapter, dedicates its last chapter to Tekki. What follows is the explanation of this *kata* given in that work along with an English translation by a translator:

> この型は、騎馬立ちと交差立ちのみで、横一直線上を左右に移動する運足に特徴があります。今まで、どのようにして使うのか不明で、空手界最大の謎とも言われてきました。この型で学ぶ分解は、超接近法であり、相手のサイドや背後に回ることを学びます。写真の単独型は、現在の松濤館の鉄騎初段とは違いますが、船越義珍先生が最初の本で掲載されたナイハンチ初段を参考にしました。鉄騎として改変された交差受けの場所は、動作を大きくしてありますが、分解は一緒だと考えています。
>
> This *kata* is characterized by footwork that moves from left to right in a lateral straight line, using only *kiba dachi* and *kosa dachi*. So far, how to use the techniques has been unknown; thus, it has been considered to be one of the biggest mysteries of the karate world. The *bunkai* learned with this *kata* is a short-distance fighting method, and one learns how to go around and behind the opponent. The *kata* shown in the photos is different from the current Tekki Shodan of Shotokan, but I referred to the Naihanchi Shodan published in Master Gichin Funakoshi's first book. The movements of the modified *kosa uke* in Tekki have been enlarged, but I believe the *bunkai* is the same.

I wish to evaluate the comments and the explanation given in the above paragraph, which is a good starting point, but I found some key ideas to be lacking. By examining my presentation and walking the path of history with me, I ask the reader to be the judge and to see what makes sense. Regardless of the decision, I hope the reader will enjoy the rediscovery of Tekki *kata* and appreciate this *kata* as it deserves to be appreciated.

I believe Tekki Shodan was placed very strategically between Heian *kata* and the "real" *kata* of Bassai Dai and Kanku Dai. Let me list and summarize the interesting and unique (and possibly mysterious) points found in Tekki *kata*. By studying these points, you will discover why this *kata* was practiced at the early stage of karate training and placed before Bassai Dai and Kanku.

1. *Kiba dachi* is the only stance used in this *kata*.

It is true that this *kata* employs only *kiba dachi* (formerly *naihanchi dachi*) except for the *kosa dachi* (交差立ち 'cross-legged stance') used when the performer shifts to the left or right side. Thus, many people believe this *kata* is a training *kata* to practice *kiba dachi* and to strengthen the legs. But, look at the *naihanchi dachi* of Funakoshi shown on page 90. Does it look as though he is squatting down low as we have been told to do lately?

His stance is not the *kiba dachi* we are familiar with. It is definitely a *naihanchi dachi*, which looks like a natural stance with a little more space between the feet You also notice that his knees are not deeply bent. It is not because he was too old—I'm guessing he was still young, maybe in his late fifties—or too lazy. There was an intentional reason why *naihanchi dachi* (later to become *kiba dachi*) was used in this *kata*. I will explain further in the latter part of this chapter as this is one of the major training points of this *kata*.

2. The *enbusen* is lateral.

All three Naihanchi *kata* (Shodan, Nidan, and Sandan) shift only to the sides and no forward or backward steps are involved. Most of the techniques seem to be delivered to the sides, though a few are delivered to the front. Thus, most people assume that the actual applications are also delivered to the sides while in *kiba dachi*, and that is the way the *bunkai* is taught by many instructors. I do not agree with this idea as I believe most of the applications are to be delivered to the front. will show some of the applications later in this chapter under the "*Bunkai*" section

3. The very first move of each *kata* goes to the right side.

Compared to the five Heian *kata*, which all start to the left side, the three Tekki *kata* all start to the right side. It is a known fact that Itosu created the Heian *kata* in the late nineteenth century. Before the Heian *kata* were invented, The Tekki *kata* were the first *kata* for practitioners of Shorin Ryu (the forefather of Shotokan) for many years. Itosu created the Heian *kata* because karate was to be adopted by the educational institution on Okinawa toward the beginning of the twentieth century.

The Ministry of Education decided to make karate a part of regular elementary and high school physical education. Apparently, Itosu thought the Tekki *kata* were too difficult and sophisticated for such an endeavor; thus, he came up with the Heian *kata*, which employed much simpler movements. He decided to start these *kata* to the left side in order to balance them with the Tekki *kata*, which start to the right side.

4. The *nami gaeshi* kick is used.

This is an interesting kick, and I was originally taught (wrongly) that the application was to block a *gedan mae geri* with my snapping foot. For many years, I struggled with this application. I could not do it effectively and have never seen anyone who could. I always blamed my poor technique or my inability to execute this technique.

Then, I learned other application ideas that made much more sense. One of them was *hiza kansetsu geri* (膝関節蹴り, 'knee joint kick'). This application is shown in the book *Hidden Karate*. Another idea was a foot sweep. The third option was a *hiza uchi uke* (膝内受け, 'inside knee block') against a *mae geri*. For *hiza uchi uke*, you use the entire knee and shin area to block against a front kick.

This application is beautifully demonstrated by Asai in the *bunkai* for Suishu *kata*, which can be viewed at this URL: www.youtube.com/watch?v=tV6cHs6WsJU.

Bunkai

Most researchers and instructors expend much effort in describing what this *kata* is all about from a historical perspective, but for *bunkai*, we do not find any specific ideas or explanations. Here I would like to share the *bunkai* I learned. But, first of all, I want to make it very clear that I am not claiming that the *bunkai* I show here is the only correct application and that all other ideas are wrong. On the contrary, my understanding is that all *kata* contain basic techniques that could be interpreted in many different ways.

Therefore, the practitioner must not get trapped in a certain fixed concept or idea when it comes to *bunkai*. However, there are appropriate and realistic applications, and I have seen some that are not realistic or useful at all. It is up to the practitioner to examine and evaluate the *bunkai* so he can determine if those applications would make sense.

I am afraid I will not be able to share all the *bunkai* of Tekki Shodan due to the limitations of the available space. I will show three *bunkai* from this *kata* to illustrate how the applications are done to the front and not necessarily to the sides. Photos of the *kata* movements from Tekki Shodan, along with their applications, are found on the following pages.

1. The first four movements of Tekki Shodan are as follows: *heisoku dachi* with *shuto kamae* (Picture 1), *kosa dachi* (Picture 2), right *fumikomi* (Picture 3), right *haishu uchi* (Picture 4).

1 2

3 4

Here is the *bunkai* for these moves:

Yoi

Application for Picture 2

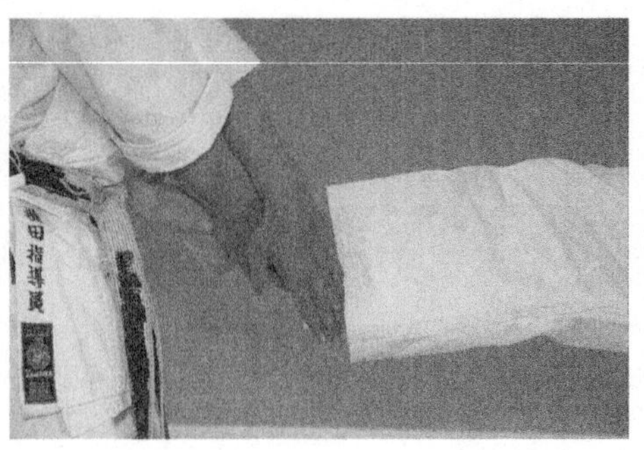

Close-up of application for Picture 2

Throw a *morote awase kaishu uke* from *kosa dachi* to block the opponent's *mae geri* (also found in Bassai Sho).

Application for Picture 3

The right *mae geri* is a counterkick.

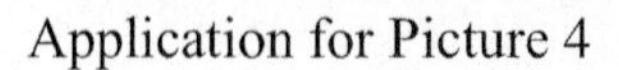

Application for Picture 4

Reverse of application for Picture 4

Throw a right *jodan haishu uchi* to the temple or a *shuto uchi* to the neck. The stance can be either a *zenkutsu dachi* or a *kiba dachi*.

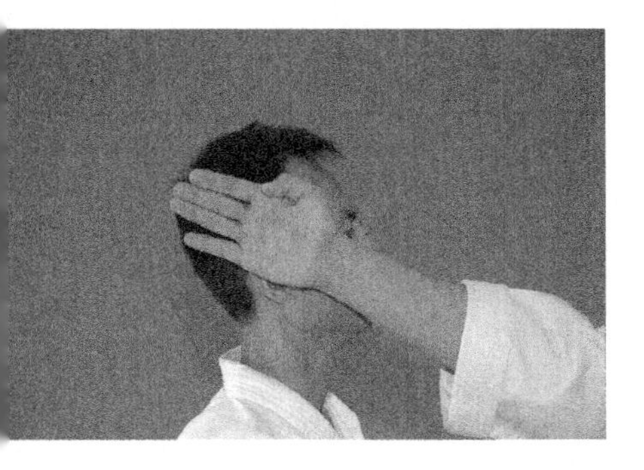

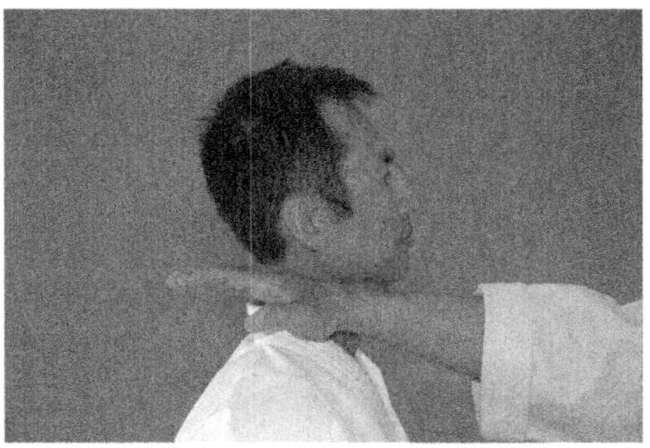

Close-up photos of possible applications

2. The next four moves of Tekki Shodan are as follows: left *enpi uchi* to right palm (Picture 5), both hands in *kamae* at right hip (Picture 6), left *gedan barai* (Picture 7), right *gyaku zuki* (Picture 8). This is a series of applications for when you are very close to the opponent.

5

6

7

8

Application for Picture 5

The right hand pulls the opponent's head closer for the left *jodan enpi uchi*.

Application for Picture 6

The left hand grabs the opponent's right sleeve, and the right hand grabs his left side to pull him in for better control.

Application for Picture 7

The left *gedan barai* is actually a move to pull the opponent's right sleeve down to get him off-balance.

Application for Picture 8

Throw the right *kagi zuki* to the opponent's head as he tries to recover his balance by raising his head up.

An alternate application of this move is a takedown. Instead of punching with the right *kagi zuki*, the right arm is placed around the body, underneath the opponent's left arm, to throw him.

This concludes Part I of Tekki *kata*. In Part II, I will continue with the *bunkai* involving the mysterious *nami gaeshi* kick. My *senpai* from forty years ago misinformed me that this technique was to block a *mae geri* aimed at my groin. So, what is the application and meaning of *nami gaeshi*? I will share the applications I learned from Sugano Sensei later. I will go over the five key objectives to aim for while practicing Tekki. These objectives have never been published before, and I hope this knowledge will reveal the true nature of Tekki *kata* and turn this "boring" *kata* into a valuable one.

Chapter Ten
第十章

Mystery Kata Tekki Shodan Part II
鉄騎初段の不思議　パート２

Let us look at the applications for the mysterious kick called *nami gaeshi*.

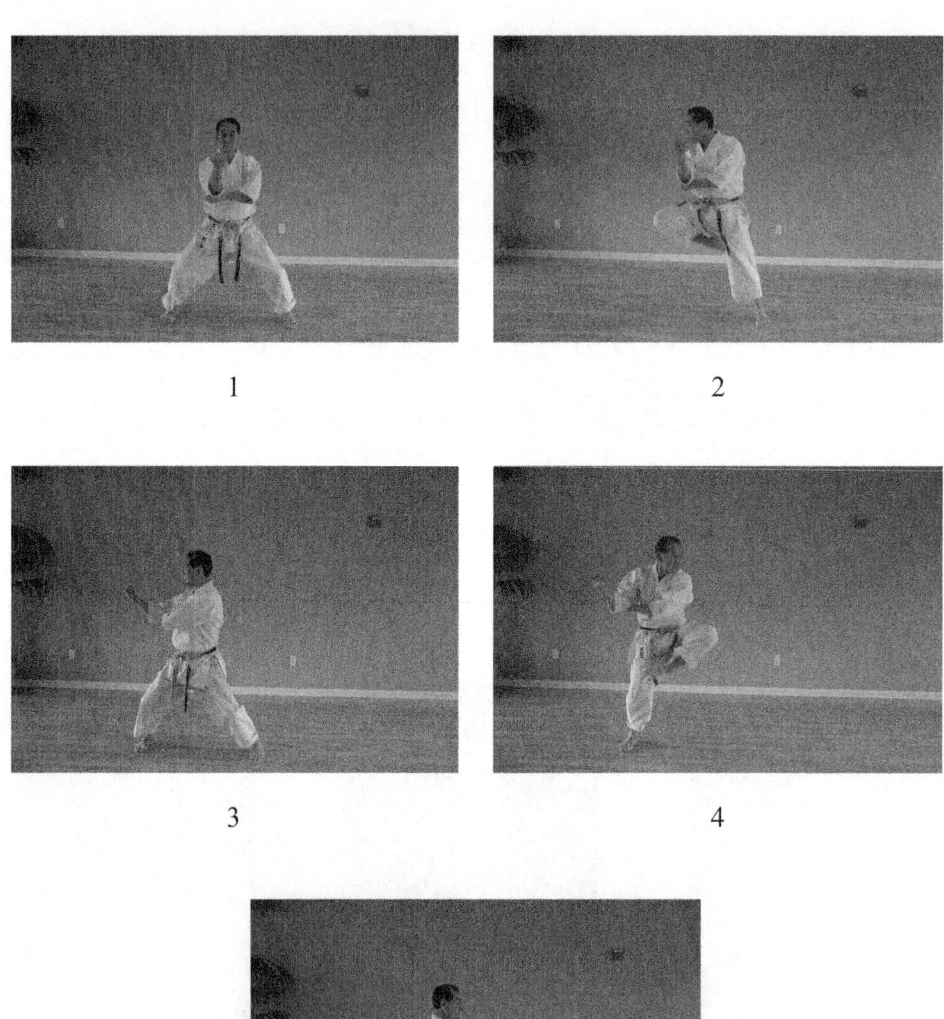

1 2

3 4

5

The *bunkai* for these moves is on the following page:

Yoi

Application for Picture 2

The *nami gaeshi* blocks the *mae geri*. Note that the knee and the entire lower-leg snap must be used to block the kick.

Application for Picture 3

Throw a right *kentsui* to the head.

Application for Picture 4

Block the right *chudan zuki* with a left *osae uke* and throw a simultaneous left *hiza geri*.

Application for Picture 5

Step in and throw a right *jodan ura zuki* to the chin.

I will now list five key objectives that should help you practice this unique *kata* correctly so that you can enjoy it more and acquire more skills from it.

1. Stance (*Kiba Dachi* or *Naihanchi Dachi*)

As I mentioned earlier, the *naihanchi dachi* was not picked for this *kata* to strengthen the leg muscles. Importantly, *naihanchi dachi* (later *kiba dachi*) was chosen because it is a fundamental stance that can easily be changed to a front stance or a back stance by shifting the center of gravity either forward or backward and pivoting the feet. Upon mastering this stance, the practitioner can easily apply its principles to different stances. Also, the practitioner learns to keep all stances narrow, even *zenkutsu dachi*.

2. Body and Center-of-Gravity Shifting

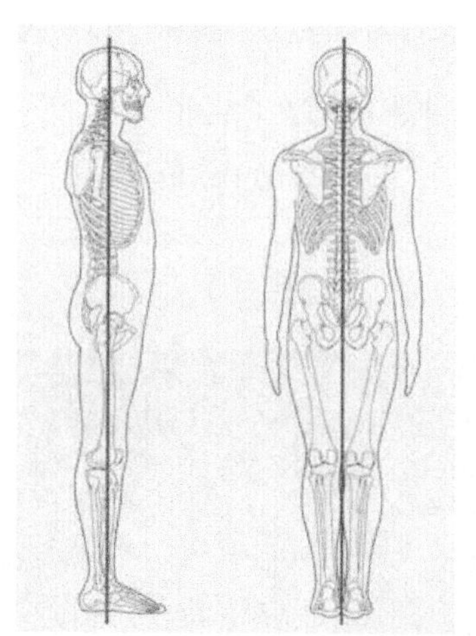

Believe it or not, the use of *kosa dachi* is probably one of the most important training points of Tekki. At the beginning of this *kata*, you are in *heisoku dachi*. Here your balance should be distributed fifty-fifty between your feet. As you shift your left foot and step over the right foot into *kosa dachi* you are simultaneously increasing the support from your right leg and decreasing the support from your left leg.

This is a simple and natural thing, so no one would disagree here, but the special attention that this motion must receive has been neglected. The support from the right leg starts at fifty percent and increases to fifty-one, fifty-two, fifty-three, etc., on up to ninety-nine percent. It almost reaches a hundred percent but not quite as your left foot still lightly touches the ground, which provides the minimum support and keeps the body balanced.

This motion is done slowly in the JKA style, which is not wrong, but the way it should be done and the reason it should be done that way have not been explained to most students. I will explain this particular point later as it deserves some close attention. The most important moment comes next.

In the next movement, you shift your support instantly from your right leg to your left, which now supports a hundred percent of the body weight (increased from one percent) since your right leg is up in the air, going for *fumikomi*. This shifting technique is the key point of this *kata*. It increases speed when shifting forward not only in regular stepping motions but also in *tsugi ashi* and *yori ashi*.

In addition, it must be mentioned that this technique is built on a fine sense of balance as well as on the use of the inner thigh muscles for quick action. If you happen to be a ninja fan, then you may know of a ninja walking method that is a crablike walk (side-stepping walk). The ninja knew the importance of using the inner thigh muscles for quick shifting.

So, students must be told to feel this slow change of balance between the left and right legs. It is slow initially (the way it is done in the first step of Tekki Shodan and Nidan), but you will eventually be able to do this center-of-gravity shift quickly. As I pointed out earlier, by learning how this gravity change feels, you will learn how to shift your body quickly and smoothly (just like a ninja).

3. Short-Distance Fighting

In an interesting article titled "Naihanchi—Karate's Most Deadly Kata?" (www.iainabernethy.co.uk/article/naihanchi-karates-most-deadly-kata), Iain Abernethy states, "There should be no doubt that close-range fighting skills are vital when it comes to defending yourself. Naihanchi provides instruction on close-range fighting; the techniques are also direct and relatively easy to apply. We can also see the integrated use of striking and grappling, which is the key to success at close range."

Shuri Te is commonly known as a long-distance fighting method, and some claim that this style is weak at short-distance fighting. I do not agree totally with this statement; however, I do agree that the basic fighting method of Shuri Te is supported mainly by long-distance stances, such as *zenkutsu dachi*, *kokutsu dachi*, and *kiba dachi*.

It is also assumed that a short-distance fighting method must use short stances, such as *neko ashi dachi* and *sanchin dachi*. It is true that short stances are more mobile, meaning that body shifting is easier in a short-distance fighting situation, such as grappling. However, it is not a surprise to find that short-distance combat can be fought effectively by using only long stances, which can be witnessed in Tekki *kata*.

4. Upper- and Lower-Body Separation Technique

Take a look at the photo to the right of Funakoshi doing Tekki. You can clearly see that he keeps his *naihanchi* stance while he is executing the arm technique to both sides by rotating the upper body by 180 degrees. In this photo, the upper half of his body is very clearly turned without compromising his stance. It almost looks as though these two halves of the body come from two different people as if it were a phony picture. His midsection must be totally flexible in order for him to execute the rotation this distinctively.

If you can do this in *kiba dachi*, then it will be easy to do a *gyaku zuki* with the hips fully turned or a reverse block (as required in Bassai Dai). This exercise also enables you to execute upper-body techniques without being influenced by the lower body and vice versa. What this means is that you will have the ability to execute upper-body techniques not only while you are in a stance but also while you are shifting or using your legs to kick or block. The reverse can also be said, which means that you will be able to use your legs independently of your upper-body movements.

5. *Bunkai* Direction

The direction of the *bunkai* can be to the sides as indicated by the movements of the *kata.* There is nothing wrong with practicing against opponents who may attack you from the sides. If you happen to face two opponents positioned at your sides, it is very probable that you will assume a *kiba dachi* and fight them accordingly. However, we should not get trapped in this concept alone as it is only one situation, and the variations of a given situation are infinite.

As I explained above, *kiba dachi* is a standard stance that can be switched to *zenkutsu dachi* or *kokutsu dachi*, depending on the distance from the opponent. So, if your stance is *zenkutsu dachi* or *kokutsu dachi*, the application is definitely against an opponent who is in front of you.

The creator of Tekki *kata* utilized only *kiba dachi* and made its *enbusen* into a straight and interestingly lateral line. For several hundred years before the Heian *kata* were invented in the late nineteenth century, Tekki was the very first *kata* taught to Shuri Te practitioners, and they would practice this *kata* alone for several years before they would move on to other *kata*, such as Bassai. Thus, it may be logical to assume that Tekki was an introductory *kata* and that the *enbusen* was purposely kept simple.

Now that you have learned the hidden techniques and objectives of this *kata*, you no longer need to limit your understanding solely to the literal interpretations. Remember that this *kata* was valued and practiced diligently by thousands of Okinawan practitioners for several centuries on the Okinawan islands. If it had not had the special values and benefits I have listed above, it most likely could not have survived over that length of time.

If this *kata* is so important, we naturally wonder why it was forced to become the required *kata* for fourth-*kyu* students testing for their brown belt. Why did Funakoshi stop emphasizing the extreme importance of this *kata* to his students? Here is my theory or an educated guess as to why this happened.

Funakoshi was a great educator, and he wanted to teach karate as a part of physical education and not as a pure martial art. He did not emphasize *kumite*, teaching mainly through *kata*. Many of his university students, I heard, dropped out or went to Okinawa on their own to learn *kumite*. So, obviously, he was not too motivated to teach the *bunkai* and applications of the *kata*, including Tekki.

I must add that he dropped many things from the original karate. The most well-known fact is that he dropped the Okinawan names from the *kata* and gave them Japanese names instead. He did this to make the names sound more Japanese so that Japanese practitioners would feel more comfortable with them. In addition, he dropped Okinawan clothing and adopted the *judogi* (柔道着) from Kodokan Judo. He did not include *kobudo* in the regular curriculum, though we see photos where he would train with a *bo*. He also de-emphasized many of the throwing techniques and *bunkai waza* so that karate would not compete against judo, which was the major martial art in mainland Japan at the time when he introduced it there.

He wanted karate to be adopted by the Japanese people as a safe sport and practiced in all high schools and universities. I am sure this caused great frustration inside him as karate was a deadly martial art, and its training objective was to make one's body as lethal as possible. He had to tone down its skills and techniques so that karate would not compete against the de facto martial art of Japan, judo. Therefore, he had to decide to drop the hidden techniques in Tekki that would turn this boring *kata* into a powerful one.

You probably wonder why Funakoshi had to worry so much about judo. I have explained this in Chapter 7: "Begin and End with Blocks," so please refer to that chapter if you have not read it yet. But, let me explain again briefly because this is a very important fact in understanding the development and history of Shotokan karate in Japan.

The founder of judo was Jigoro Kano, and he had a tremendous amount of political power and authority in the fields of education and athletics in Japan for many years between the late nineteenth and early twentieth centuries. He was not only the *kancho* (館長, 'chairman') of the Kodokan, the headquarters of judo, but also the first International Olympic Committee (IOC) member in Japan. For many years, he was the principal of several high schools and universities, which naturally made him a renowned educator with much credibility and respect. To go against him or judo in the early twentieth century would have been suicide.

Funakoshi had just moved from Okinawa (an island that most Japanese did not then consider to be a part of Japan) and did not have a network or any supporters in Tokyo. He was living in a custodian's apartment in a dormitory of one of the universities. His job was to teach a "strange" martial art called *karate* (唐手, 'Chinese hand'), which was almost totally unknown to Japan at that time. It is easy to imagine that he needed to get on Kano's good side and form some kind of alliance with judo. So, now the reader will have a better understanding of the strong influence judo had on the development of karate in Japan during the first half of the twentieth century.

Let me finish this chapter with a well-known story about Choki Motobu (本部朝基, 1870–1944 [photo left]), the very famous Shuri Te master from Okinawa. Motobu's nickname was *Saru* (猿), literally meaning 'monkey'. The following is a short story about how he got this nickname.

On Okinawa, in those days, in order for karate practitioners to try out their skills, they held unofficial street-corner matches at night. There was a certain open space where they would meet on weekend nights just as modern-day boys meet for street drag races.

The story goes that after Motobu continually won many matches, no one would dare challenge him any longer. So, he would hide up on top of the roof of a nearby house and watch the matches that were being held below. Toward the end of the matches, when he could determine the best fighter of the group, he would jump down from the rooftop and challenge that person. The way he climbed up and down the roof made him look like a monkey, so he was called *Bushi Saru* (武士猿, 'Samurai Monkey').

So, Motobu was one of the best fighters that Okinawa produced, and he claimed that Tekki was the only *kata* he needed to practice. We know that this claim is an exaggeration, and he, in fact, knew other *kata*. But, it is true that he stressed the importance of Naihanchi (Tekki) *kata* with this kind of statement.

Do you still believe that Tekki is simply a requirement to become a brown belt? If you currently ignore this *kata* in your regular training agenda, don't you think now is a good time for you to bring it back into your training repertoire? I am sure it will help you learn the "secret" techniques of Tekki, and that will result in some significant improvements in your overall karate performance.

Chapter Eleven
第十一章

Hangetsu
半月形

Is Hangetsu *kata* a missing link to Naha Te? The late Steve Cattle (of the UK) wrote an educational and much-needed article on Hangetsu titled "Hangetsu: the Neglected Kata of Shotokan" in Issue 47 (May 1996) of *Shotokan Karate Magazine*. Here he pointed out that this *kata* was most unpopular and claimed, "I feel it is a very neglected *kata*, generally because of the difficulty in performing the turns, the stance and its lack of beauty." He concluded that the biggest reason this *kata* is unpopular is due to the difficulty of its turns and its stance, *hangetsu dachi*, stating, "The difficulty is in the turn, which is why I think it is neglected in competition as well as the actual stance difficulty." I agree with most of his claims, but I am afraid he missed some key points. If you investigate the origin of this unique *kata*, you will discover the hidden history and the deep mysteries behind it.

Even though Shuri Te and Naha Te do not share all of the same *kata*, Hangetsu (Seisan/Seishan) is one exception. This *kata* is found in almost all styles, including Wado Ryu, Shito Ryu, Goju Ryu, Uechi Ryu, Shorin Ryu, Ryuei Ryu, etc. I will attempt to put the facts together and make necessary comparisons to come up with the answers to many questions. By sharing these findings, I hope the reader will come to a new appreciation and understanding when he performs this unique and valuable *kata*.

There is another article that is definitely worth reading, which is found in Issue 49 (November 1996) of *Shotokan Karate Magazine* and was written by John Cheetham, the chief editor of the magazine. The title is "Inside Tension Stances," and it has the subtitle "Sanchin Dachi, Neko Ashi Dachi, Hangetsu Dachi." It is a three-page article explaining what these inside-tension stances are and how they are constructed. It touches on a subject that is not frequently addressed, and I recommend that all Shotokan practitioners read it if they have not already.

Unfortunately, there is no detailed information about *hangetsu dachi* and its unique nature mentioned or described in this article. However, I cannot blame the author at all. He probably has a set of all the karate textbooks, such as *Dynamic Karate*, *Karate Do Kyohan*, and *Best Karate*, where he can find only the steps of Hangetsu *kata* and not much else.

In fact, we find very little information on how to do this *kata* properly or on the details of *hangetsu dachi*. The author writes, "*Hangetsu dachi* is described in most books and by most instructors as a longer version of *sanchin dachi* with all the same points as *sanchin*." This is how it skips any detailed description of *hangetsu dachi*. In this chapter, I will attempt to bring out the hidden facts about this *kata* from history and compare it to the versions of the other *ryuha* (流派, 'styles') to fill in the gaps.

The reader will agree by now that Hangetsu *kata*, along with *hangetsu dachi*, is unpopular. I wonder if you are aware that this is the most mysterious of all the Shotokan *kata*. You might have already discarded this *kata* as a "boring" *kata*, so you may be questioning why I am making a big deal about it. I invite the reader to travel along with me and discover some interesting facts in karate history.

After investigating this *kata*'s history, the background of Funakoshi's training on Okinawa, and the major "improvements" made by Nakayama, I must say that the depth of this *kata*'s mysteriousness surpasses that of Tekki. As far as I can tell, with the exception of the late Steve Cattle's article, my research on Hangetsu is the first ever, and it reveals the reason that this *kata* must not become a forgotten one.

When I first learned of Hangetsu *kata*, I considered it to be an easy one that was reserved for seniors. When my original instructor in Kobe, Jun Sugano, demonstrated Hangetsu with *ibuki* in the early eighties, I did not think much of it—or, truthfully, I did not understand it. When I saw him demonstrating this *kata* with that breathing method, I thought maybe he was sick and was having difficulty breathing.

Like a typical Japanese instructor, Sugano did not explain *ibuki* or the purpose this *kata* to us. I actually do not remember him teaching us this *kata* at all in the dojo. I am sure he taught it to the senior instructors, but for the junior instructors, he chose other faster-tempo *kata*, such as Kanku, Enpi, and Unsu.

Many years later, Asai explained *ibuki* breathing and its effect on the stance. Then (and only then), it finally made sense to me. Boy, you talk about a slow learner; it only took me twenty years to see it. This technique seems to have been nearly lost among Shotokan practitioners. Only Kanazawa and a few other instructors mention the importance of breathing in this *kata*, but none of them explain the full meaning of *ibuki* and Hangetsu. Consequently, the whole story of the missing link between Shotokan and Naha Te has never been revealed. There is much more there than meets the eye.

Before we investigate the "mysterious" points of Hangetsu, I want to bring to your attention two unique facts about this *kata* that have not been discussed much in the past.

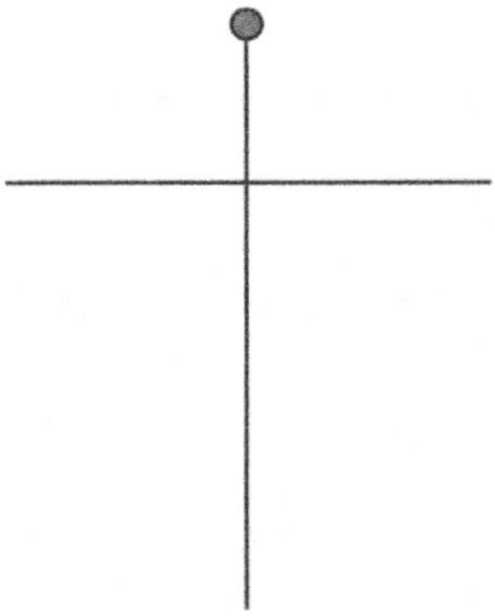

The first fact is that Hangetsu's *enbusen* is rare in that it stays basically on one medial line running forward and backward. There are *chudan uchi uke* and *nihon zuki* sequences in the middle of the *kata* that extend to the left and right, but they only have one *yori ashi* step of deviation. So, we can say that it stays within one medial line, and this idea is similar to that of Gankaku (also on a medial line) and Tekki (on a lateral line). When an *enbusen* is simple, it means the *kata* creator did this on purpose. He eliminated complex footwork in order to emphasize certain techniques, typically a stance or several stances, for training purposes.

Tekki has at least three major purposes: (1) strengthening the legs with the low *kiba dachi*, (2) mastering the technique of transferring the center of gravity by shifting the body sideways (in unnatural directions), and (3) increasing upper-body flexibility. The training objective of Gankaku is also very clear: it trains your balancing ability with *tsuru ashi dachi* and its many dynamic body rotations.

Then, what are the specific objectives of Hangetsu *kata*? There are several points, and this chapter will review them as we investigate the points that make

Hangetsu very unique.

The second fact is that all styles have this *kata* (Hangetsu or Seisan/Seishan). It is very interesting to note that all traditional styles of both Shuri Te (e.g., Wado Ryu and Shorin Ryu) and Naha Te (e.g., Shito Ryu, Goju Ryu, Uechi Ryu, and Ryuei Ryu) have this *kata* under the name of either *Seisan* or *Seishan*. Shotokan has no other *kata* that overlap with the Naha Te styles, so Hangetsu *kata* is the rare bridge to Naha Te.

Seisan and *Seishan* are Okinawan words that mean 'thirteen'. Naha Te styles call it *Jusanho* (十三歩, 'thirteen steps') or *Jusante* (十三手, 'thirteen hands' or 'thirteen techniques'). Funakoshi changed the name to *Hangetsu* sometime in the late twenties or early thirties while he was trying to make karate more Japanese. One of the contributions he made was to replace the Okinawan *kata* names, which were incomprehensible to the Japanese population, with more Japanese-sounding names.

The fact that all styles share this same *kata* is, needless to say, tremendously useful and valuable as it allows us to compare each style's version of the *kata*. This work will hopefully tell us a lot about Shotokan and its link to Naha Te. There are three interesting points that make Hangetsu *kata* a very unique and mysterious *kata*:

- It contains *hangetsu dachi.*
- It uses slow movements in the first portion.
- It contains the forgotten instruction of *ibuki* breathing.

Hangetsu Dachi

Most readers know that the name *Hangetsu* (半月, 'half-moon') was adopted because the steps in this *kata* are inwardly circular. In Shotokan, we emphasize the outward stances, such as *kiba dachi*, *zenkutsu dachi*, and *kokutsu dachi*; thus, inner-tension stances, including *hangetsu dachi*, are not popular. In fact, the inward stances were not a part of my regular *kihon* practice during my JKA days.

I remember clearly when I first learned this stance in the early seventies. My *senpai* said, "Get in your *zenkutsu dachi*. Now, turn the front foot inward by thirty degrees. Then, squeeze the knees in." Wow, it was a very strange feeling, and I had difficulty staying in the stance. I was worried that I might hurt my knees by pulling them in so much.

Another problem was that it was difficult to hold *hangetsu dachi* during the first ten slow moves leading up to the *morote shuto gedan uke* (or *uchi*). As I did my upper-body techniques, I tended to forget the inner tension of the legs. I remember clearly the serious challenge of holding *hangetsu dachi* throughout this *kata*.

Below is a photo of our *hangetsu dachi* with a corresponding diagram (Picture A). This is the *hangetsu dachi* form I learned many years ago, and I suspect this is the way the reader has been instructed or is now instructing his students.

A. Shotokan *hangetsu dachi*

In Volume 7 of *Best Karate*, Nakayama writes the following for *hangetsu dachi*:

> Slightly narrower than the front stance, both feet are turned in toward the line connecting the insteps and both knees are twisted inward. It is important that both heels and outside edges of the feet (*sokuto*) be firmly planted.

In *Dynamic Karate*, he explains *hangetsu dachi* as

> a stance midway between the front stance and the hour glass stance. The placing of the feet is almost the same as in the front stance but the distance between the feet in *hangetsu* is shorter. The method of forcing the knees inward, however, is similar to the hour-glass stance. This stance is useful for both attack and defense, but tends to be favored for defense.

As I progressed to higher rank and learned all twenty-six JKA *kata*, I realized that we find *neko ashi dachi* and *sanchin dachi* in other *kata* (e.g., Nijushiho [二十四歩], Unsu, and Wankan). On the other hand, *hangetsu dachi* is nowhere to be found except in Hangetsu *kata*. As my research extended to other styles, I found that no other style has *hangetsu dachi*!

Initially, I investigated how the Naha Te styles do their *kata* as they focus on inward-tension stances. I discovered that all of them use *sanchin dachi* in Seisan (see Pictures B and C below).

B. Goju Ryu Seisan

C. Shito Ryu Seisan

Wado Ryu (和道流) is a spin-off style of Shotokan, and their *kata* is called *Seishan*. The *seishan* stance, which is shown with a corresponding diagram below (Picture D), is similar to *hangetsu dachi* (front foot turned inward and knees pulled in), but it is much shorter and is actually closer to *sanchin dachi*. In fact, some Wado Ryu dojo websites describe *seishan dachi* as being the same as *sanchin dachi*.

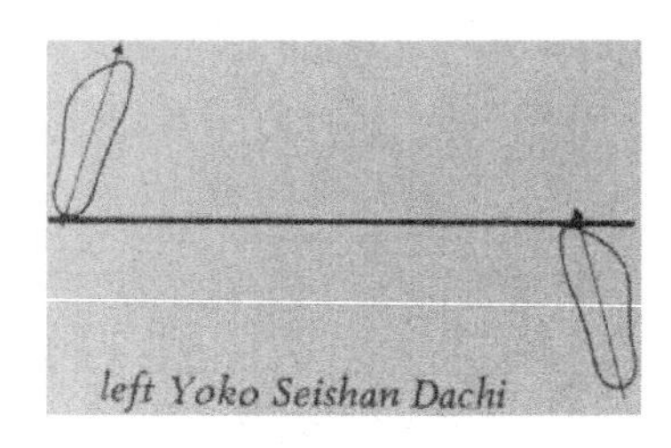

D. Wado Ryu *seishan dachi*

Now we have to check the original Shuri Te style from which Shotokan originated. Shorin Ryu (少林流, 小林流, or 松林流) is the major style of Shuri Te, and the stance it uses in Seisan *kata* is shown below (Picture E).

The stance almost looks like *shiko dachi*. The rear leg is very much bent, and the knee is even pushed outward. Obviously, they use outward-tension stances in their Seisan *kata*.

E. Shorin Ryu Seisan

Let's look at the Shotokai's version now. The Shotokai adopted the new name, *Hangetsu*, when Funakoshi changed it. The photo shown below (Picture F) shows a move (*morote gedan kakiwake*) from Hangetsu.

This is the stance they use in Hangetsu (see *Karate Do Kyohan*), and we see that it is very similar to that of Shorin Ryu with the rear knee pushed outward almost like *shiko dachi* or *sochin dachi*. Based on the strong similarity of Shorin Ryu's Seisan *kata* to the Shotokai's Hangetsu *kata*, we can easily determine that the former was a forefather of the latter.

F. Shotokai stance

Here is a video clip of Hangetsu as performed by a Shotokai practitioner: www.youtube.com/watch?v=FvULsvwrxYs. The film quality is very poor, but we can see the stances very clearly.

Given that the Shotokai is a devoted follower of Funakoshi, I do not know why they kept the outward stance instead of following the change of stance that Funakoshi made. I would like to receive input from Shotokai practitioners or anyone who has investigated this area in order to solve this mystery.

After reviewing all of these styles' stances, we can conclude that neither the Shuri Te styles nor the inward-stance-centric Naha Te styles have the *hangetsu dachi* (an inward stance) we know of today. So, we now want to know why *hangetsu dachi* stands alone in Shotokan among all the styles. This is a big question, and I am aware that my answer can be very controversial.

Funakoshi is believed to have learned karate from two masters: Anko Itosu and Anko Azato. Funakoshi's main source of karate techniques was from Shuri Te, and some claim that he did not acquire many of the Naha Te techniques. This claim does make sense as Shotokan stances are mainly long outward stances, and its fighting style is definitely focused on long distance.

For most Shuri Te experts, this was sufficient as they considered Shuri Te to be the traditional and authentic Okinawan martial art of *te* (or *ti*). Why did Shuri Te focus on long-distance fighting? For that answer, we will need to go into the history of ancient Okinawan fighting.

It is a fact that iron ore has always been rare on Okinawa. The ancient Okinawans could not produce steel to make swords and other steel weapons as the Japanese could. This is why most of the Okinawan *kobudo* weapons, such as the *bo* (棒), nunchaku (ヌンチャク), *tonfa* (トンファー), and even boat oars, are made of wood. Swords were available only to the high-ranking *bushi* (武士, 'warrior' or 'samurai'); therefore, obviously, most *bushi* had to develop long-distance methods for fighting against opponents with weapons.

The Naha Te styles, such as Goju Ryu and Uechi Ryu, are much newer as the founders of those styles traveled to China to learn mainly *hakutsuru ken* (White Crane kung fu) in the nineteenth century. Because of its short history, the credibility of Naha Te was still not there in the early twentieth century, and I can see why Funakoshi did not train deeply in the Naha Te styles.

Knowing that Funakoshi was an educator and a dedicated *karateka*, I am sure he tried to incorporate some of the ideas from Naha Te. He must have known the importance of inward stances and *ibuki* breathing, which are the two core principles of Naha Te. *Sanchin dachi* is used by Naha Te, but he wanted a longer stance for Shotokan, which is a long-distance fighting system. Therefore, he created a long stance with inward tension, a combination of *zenkutsu dachi* and *sanchin dachi*. That new creation was *hangetsu dachi*.

Slow Movements

The first ten movements—the number may be different, depending on how you count the movements—from the first left *chudan uchi ude uke* up to the *morote shuto gedan uke* (or *uchi*), are performed very slowly (as in tai chi), and the stepping movement must coordinate with the *uchi ude uke* techniques. This is tremendously unique among Shotokan *kata*, and not much explanation has been given as to why we must perform it this way. It is commonly explained that it is a coordination exercise like the first two slow movements of Heian Yondan. But, why do we have ten of these slow movements in succession? There must be a serious reason, but this has never been fully addressed by anyone.

Because of these "easy" moves, this *kata* is mistakenly considered to be a *kata* for old practitioners. In addition, Hangetsu is not a popular choice at tournaments. On the other hand, we frequently see it performed by old masters as a demonstration piece. I recall observing demos of Hangetsu often in the seventies and eighties in Japan and the U.S. I remember seeing Nishiyama do a demo of Hangetsu with an impressive *bunkai* in Manhattan, New York, more than thirty years ago. Enoeda Sensei was there, too, and he did another *kata* demo.

We must consider further why the masters would pick this *kata* for demonstrations. Let us compare the tempo, particularly that of the first portion of this *kata*, among the versions of the other styles.

Wado Ryu (Shuri Te)

Here is a video clip of Hironori Otsuka doing Seishan: www.youtube.com/watch?v=ckH_3iIRKwg. Wado Ryu is a style that is very close to Shotokan as its founder, Hironori Otsuka (大塚博紀, 1892–1982), was one of Funakoshi's disciples.

After reviewing the video clip of Seishan by Otsuka, it can easily be recognized that this is the same *kata*. One of the differences is that Otsuka continues the slow movements after the *morote shuto gedan uke* all the way up until the sequences of *chudan uchi ude uke* and *nihon zuki*, which are done quickly. Obviously, Otsuka chose to take the slow movements more aggressively than Funakoshi, and I believe Otsuka found that the objective of this *kata* was important enough to extend these slow movements.

Okinawan Shorin Ryu (Shuri Te)

Here is a video clip of Okinawan Seibukan Seisan: www.youtube.com/watch?v=LFSnV7s_5i0.

The foot movement is an inward crescent shape done slowly, but the arm movements are done in a fast motion. Another interesting thing is that after the right *gyaku zuki*, a quick right *chudan uchi ude uke* is done from the *gyaku* position (while in a left *zenkutsu dachi*). Then, there is a step forward into a right *shiko dachi* without moving the arms (the step being done somewhat slowly). After the right *shiko dachi* is complete, a left *gyaku zuki* is executed strongly and quickly This sequence is repeated one more time.

Seibukan keeps its outward-stance tradition by finishing this *kata* with a *zenkutsu dachi* (an outward stance). It is interesting to note that Shotokan, on the other hand, finishes with a *neko ashi dachi* (an inward stance).

Goju Ryu (Naha Te)

This is the most famous style of the Naha Te group. The major difference between Goju Ryu and most other styles is that Goju Ryu uses the heavier *ibuk* breathing method (explained later in this chapter) during the execution of the *kata* As far as the first ten moves or so are concerned, the *kata* starts by slowly stepping into a right *sanchin dachi* and getting into a *morote uchi kakiwake* position which looks like having both arms in a *chudan uchi uke* position. In this move there is coordination between the stance and the arm movement. Then, one arm is slowly pulled back to the hip position before it delivers a *chudan zuki* followed by a *chudan uchi ude uke* in rapid succession. These moves are quite different from Hangetsu. The next step into a left *sanchin dachi* is made at regular speed, and both arms are held up in a *kakiwake* position. Here is a video of Goju Ryu's version of Seisan: www.youtube.com/watch?v=Ba2qjV0GFa4.

Shito Ryu (Naha Te)

Shito Ryu is a sister style of Shotokan as the founders of both styles had a common Okinawan teacher, Anko Itosu. However, Shito Ryu's Seisan *kata* is quite different from Hangetsu and is much closer to Goju Ryu's Seisan.

Below are some videos of the versions of two other Naha Te styles, Ryuei Ryu (劉衛流) and Uechi Ryu (上地流), for further comparison:

Ryuei Ryu Seisan: www.youtube.com/watch?v=vTtRyNjA2eY
Uechi Ryu Seisan: www.youtube.com/watch?v=7zXmNYXxRO0

The conclusion is that the other styles show some slow moves in their Seisan *kata*, but none of them do the successive slow movements found in Hangetsu. So, where does this idea come from? To answer this, we need to view a video clip of the Goju Kai's Sanchin *kata* as performed by Goshi Yamaguchi (山口剛史, 1942–): www.youtube.com/watch?v=EpEVNUIkVx8.

When you compare Seisan *kata* and Sanchin *kata*, interestingly, you will notice the peculiar fact that the slow foot and arm movements of the first three or four steps are identical to those of Hangetsu except that the foot and arm movements in Sanchin are done with *ibuki* breathing.

Funakoshi must have known the good points of Naha Te and wanted to incorporate the coordination of the inner-tension stance and the movement of the arms and legs with the breathing into his teaching. The Naha Te styles have Sanchin *kata* for this purpose, but he did not pick that *kata*—the reason will be explained later. Instead, he chose a similar *kata*, which conveniently had a longer stance: Seishan.

Funakoshi wanted to create a unique *kata* to supplement the Shotokan *kata* syllabus. We can see Funakoshi's wish to create a new *kata* in his act of naming it something completely different. As I have explained before, *Seisan* or *Seishan* means 'thirteen'. We already have several *kata* with numbers, such as Jutte ('ten hands') and Nijushiho ('twenty-four steps'). He could have named it *Jusante* or *Jusanho*, but he didn't do this. Instead, he came up with a completely new and unrelated name: *Hangetsu*.

It is recorded that the reason for this new name came from the crescent-shaped movements of the arms and feet. However, the crescent step is not unique to *hangetsu dachi* as we step in a similar way when we do *zenkutsu dachi*, so this does not make sense. I must say that there was a hidden motivation in Funakoshi, which has never been revealed before.

Ibuki Breathing

There are two important basics to the Naha Te styles. One is Sanchin *kata*, and it is done together with the other, *ibuki*. The latter is a very important breathing method among Naha Te styles, such as Goju Ryu, Isshin Ryu (一心流), and Uechi Ryu, as well as Kyokushinkai (極真会)—Masutatsu Oyama (大山倍達, 1923–1994) claimed in his book that he had learned it from Goju Ryu.

Sanchin *kata* is done with *ibuki* in order to learn the complex tension and relaxation of the inner body muscles. This exercise supposedly makes the practitioner's body more sustainable against hits from opponents. During training, a sensei or a *senpai* will check the degree of correct tension by hitting or kicking the practitioner on many different parts of his body, including some *kyusho* (急

所, 'vital points'), such as the solar plexus and the groin, while he is performing Sanchin *kata*.

The Naha Te styles are based on a short-distance fighting system. In a short-distance fight, you tend to receive multiple hits instead of the single knockout punch or kick that is used by Shotokan, a long-distance system. So, this exercise is to increase the defensive ability of Naha Te practitioners.

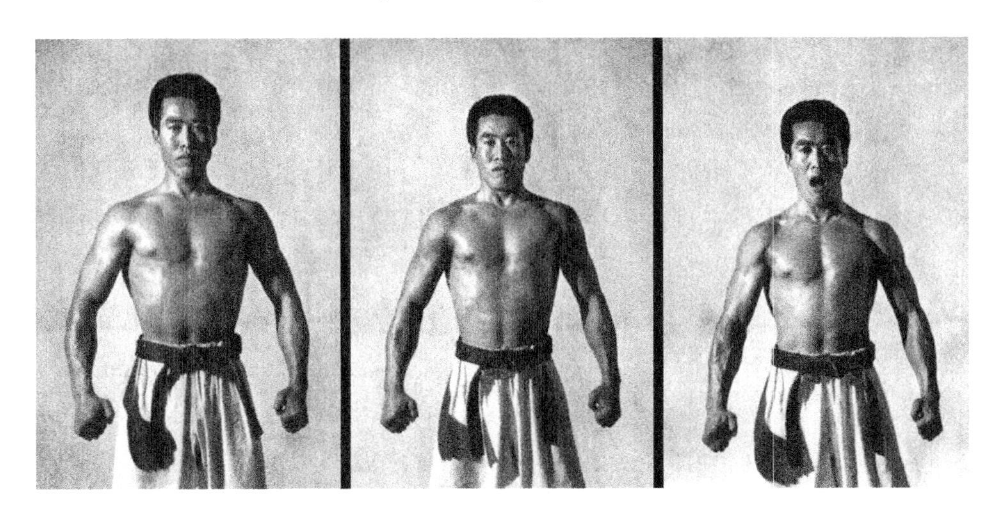

Why didn't Funakoshi choose to incorporate Sanchin *kata*, the fundamental *kata* of the Naha Te styles, into the Shotokan syllabus? I think there were three key reasons.

The first reason is that Sanchin *kata* is done with *sanchin dachi*, a short stance, and he felt that a Shotokan *kata* needed a longer stance. So, he invented an inward stance, *hangetsu dachi*, by mixing *zenkutsu dachi* with *sanchin dachi*. As I have mentioned before, this stance is Funakoshi's original, and this is the very reason the *hangetsu* stance is not found in any other style.

The second reason is that he did not accept the heavy sound of *ibuki*. Shuri Te's breathing method is a silent one. This is because he believed, as did all Shuri Te practitioners, that fighters must hide their breathing and keep it as unnoticeable as possible, especially upon inhalation (when the body becomes relaxed and thus weak).

He disliked *ibuki*'s heavy breathing sound even though this exercise was used only for body-tension exercises. Consequently, Funakoshi adopted the breathing method of a different *kata* (Seishan) and did not emphasize the heavy and noisy breathing of *ibuki* or explain it in his books. He did teach it to his disciples as an essential exercise, which has been lost, and there is proof that Nakayama learned it, which I will show later.

The third reason is that Funakoshi did not approve of the practice of actually beating the practitioners as was exercised in Goju Ryu and Uechi Ryu. His training consisted mainly of *kata* and a little *kumite*. Actually, many university students were not satisfied with his training methods, and they secretly practiced *jiyu kumite*. When Funakoshi found out about this at one of the universities, he got so upset that he resigned from his teaching post. When he later grudgingly permitted the students to engage in some controlled *kumite* (e.g., *ippon kumite*, *sanbon kumite*, etc.), he demanded that they use the *sundome* (寸止め, 'one-inch stop') noncontact method. Based on this, we can easily tell that Funakoshi did not like the idea of an exercise that would condition the body by using actual punches and kicks.

In conclusion, Funakoshi modified Sanchin *kata* in order to create Hangetsu *kata* because he did not want to adopt its short stance, its noisy breathing practice of *ibuki*, or its body-conditioning exercise.

From the very beginning, this breathing method was not emphasized to many Shotokan instructors. Consequently, instruction on breathing and how the legs are to be tensed is not provided these days when Hangetsu *kata* is taught. Even if a breathing method is mentioned, the instruction is often too simplistic: "Breathe in long" or "Breathe in slowly."

The techniques of inhalation and exhalation must be taught properly on each and every move. Some parts of the breathing and movements are more complex, but I will not go into the details in this chapter. I suggest that interested readers do their own research and possibly find an instructor who can teach the *ibuki* breathing method.

There is another big question we must answer: why is there a gap between how Funakoshi's stance looked in the 1920s and how we do it now? Below are some vintage photos of him doing Hangetsu (Seishan) in the 1920s.

In the English version of *Karate Do Kyohan* as translated by Ohshima, Funakoshi mentions the following about Hangetsu *kata*:

> This form is of the Shōrei school, which stresses in particular the training and development of the body. These movements are executed slowly and display application of power at the critical points of each technique. This fact should be kept in mind during the form, especially in the manner of application of strength and in the tensing of the legs.

The stance in the photos to the right looks like a short *zenkutsu dachi* and is actually very similar to the stance that Wado Ryu's Otsuka showed in his *kata*. So, Otsuka did follow the *seishan dachi* as Funakoshi taught it in the 1920s.

Originally, as seen in the photos, Funakoshi did not require the knees to be pulled in as we do now. It was not necessary as he must have taught this *kata* with *ibuki*-like breathing. If you do *ibuki*, you will find that the inside of the legs is tightened and that the tension in the lower stomach area (*tanden* [丹田]) increases, especially upon exhalation; therefore, your legs are naturally pulled in.

Unfortunately, the *ibuki* part of this *kata* was disregarded and forgotten by most instructors. I believe this is the main reason Hangetsu *kata* became so unpopular.

Nakayama was the core person who created JKA karate after it was founded in 1947. He was a well-educated person who brought a "scientific" approach to karate. A lot of the explanations of karate techniques in his books included scientific mechanisms such as gears and levers.

I am sure he learned *ibuki* from Funakoshi, but he also de-emphasized it jus as Funakoshi did. He considered such a breathing method to be confusing to Sho tokan as he also believed in a quiet breathing method. *Ibuki* creates internal muscl tension, which is externally invisible. Therefore, Nakayama had to choose anothe method to bring the knees inward to create an inner-tension stance.

When practitioners disregarded *ibuki* breathing in this *kata*, they naturally ha difficulty keeping the inward tension in their legs. Thus, an exaggerated pulling o the knees was added to *hangetsu dachi* in order to keep the inward tension. Bu this change only served to hide an important ingredient of this unique *kata*.

Though he dropped *ibuki*, he still considered the coordination of the move with the breathing to be important in this *kata*. So, in Volume 7 of *Best Karate* he writes, "Fast and slow techniques, hand and foot movements coordinated wit breathing and sliding the feet in arc shaped movements are characteristic of thi *kata*."

If you have this book, take a close look a the photo on the cover (photo left). Here you ca clearly observe that Nakayama has his mout slightly open. There is a hint here that he is ex ecuting an exhaled breath with his mouth ope during his Hangetsu *kata* performance. Unfortu nately, however, we cannot find any directions o instructions on how to exercise breathing in thi book or any of his books.

It was very ingenious of Funakoshi to brin in the Naha Te techniques in the way he arrange it. He created a Shotokan-specific inward-tensio stance: *hangetsu dachi*. He also modified the Seishan *kata* of Shuri Te to move lik Sanchin *kata* with a touch of a breathing exercise, one of the main components o Naha Te technique.

However, I am sure the reader will agree that it was a very unfortunate devel opment (or regression) for Shotokan to have disregarded the core concept of the breathing exercise in the process. Consequently, we almost lost the art of heavy breathing and of coordination of the inner body muscles taught in this *kata*. So, we have to admit that the tragedy is that we lost this important connection to Naha Te techniques. This is why I call Hangetsu the missing link to Naha Te.

Hangetsu dachi

Sanchin dachi

Chapter Twelve
第十二章

Bujutsu or Budo
武術か武道か

Are you practicing karate as *bujutsu* (武術) or *budo* (武道)? Do you care? I hope you do. I believe it does matter, and we must ask all karate practitioners and instructors this question. Unfortunately, many of them do not care. Even if they do, they either fail to understand the differences or are too lazy to research these concepts. Let's look at some popular reasons for which people take up and practice karate:

- Self-defense
- Health/physical conditioning
- Stress reduction/mental wellness
- Competition/tournaments

All of these reasons are good and respectable ones. We must not pass judgment on any of these reasons or regard any of them as being better than the others. Though I am glad to see people practicing karate for whatever reason, I have a strong concern regarding the current trend toward a tremendously high degree of participation in tournament activities, especially by children and youth.

In fact, too much emphasis is put on winning. Participants are told to do whatever is necessary to win matches. They are encouraged to do things such as use only certain techniques that are easier to score with, bend the rules, do illegal things (e.g., hide techniques from the judges), change *kata* moves to look "fancy," etc. Their ultimate goal is to win without paying much attention to anything else, and that is the essence of *bujutsu*, 'martial arts'. Sixteenth-century Japan was a period of war, and those who lived during that era cared only about the best swordsmanship in order to survive in battle.

Well then, what is the difference between *bujutsu* and *budo*? I believe half of the problem comes from the fact that many of us do not have a clear understanding of the differences between the two terms and concepts. Most of us consider them to be the same or believe that they are interchangeable. This is the gravest misconception, and it is where the serious problem begins.

I wanted to see if I could find a definition for *bujutsu* in the dictionary. So, I checked for it on *Merriam-Webster*, but, strangely, I could not find it. Under *bujutsu*, it said, "The word you've entered isn't in the dictionary." Instead, it listed words such as *jujutsu* and *ninjutsu*. So, I checked for *budo*. According to that dictionary, *budo* are "the Japanese martial arts (such as karate, aikido, and kendo)."

I then tried to see if I could find another source where the difference between *bujutsu* and *budo* was explained. Believe it or not, I did find a book that discusses the meaning and usage of the terms *bujutsu* and *budo*. It is Karl Friday's book *Legacies of the Sword: the Kashima-Shinryū and Samurai Martial Culture* (University of Hawai'i Press, 1997). It also compares another term, *bugei* (武芸), but we will not discuss that as it is not directly connected to our discussion here. Here are some excerpts from Mr. Friday's work:

> The meaning and usage of the terms *budō*, *bujutsu*, and *bugei* as appellations for the martial arts of Japan are subjects of considerable confusion and misinformation among practitioners and aficionados of these arts—Japanese as well as Western. Among modern authorities in Japan the terms have acquired a more or less conventional usage adopted mainly to facilitate discussion of the multiple goals and purposes of combative training: *Bujutsu* (warrior skills) describes the various Japanese martial disciplines in their original function as arts of war; *budō* (the warrior's way) denotes the process by which the study of *bujutsu* becomes a means to self-development and self-realization; and *bugei* (warrior arts) is a catchall term for the traditional Japanese military sciences,

> embracing both *bujutsu* and *budō*.
>
> It must be stressed, however, that such precise usage is modern—adopted for analytical purposes—not traditional. Projecting it backward into earlier times, as much literature on Japanese martial art does, is anachronous.
>
> Western texts on Japanese fighting arts often assert that during the Tokugawa period (A.D. 1600–1868) martial art masters began replacing the suffix *jutsu*, meaning "art" or "skill," with *dō*, meaning "way" or "path," in the names of their disciplines, to distinguish the sublime from the purely technical applications and purposes of martial art. Thus *kenjutsu*, "the art of swordsmanship," became *kendō*, "the way of the sword"; *bujutsu*, "the martial skills," became *budō*, "the martial way"; and so on. The historical record, however, does not support this conclusion...
>
> *Budō* and *bujutsu* came into fashion during the medieval and early modern periods. *Budō*, which appeared in print at least as early as the thirteenth century, seems to have been rather ambiguous in meaning until the Tokugawa period, when it sometimes carried special connotations. Nineteenth-century scholar and philosopher Aizawa Yasushi differentiated *budō* from *bugei* in the following manner: "The arts of the sword, spear, bow and saddle are the *bugei*; to know etiquette and honor, to preserve the way of the gentleman, to strive for frugality, and thus become a bulwark of the state, is *budō*" (Tominaga 1971). For at least some Tokugawa-period writers, in other words, *budō* had far broader implications than it does today, designating what modern authors often anachronistically call *bushidō*—that is, the code of conduct, rather than the military arts, of the warrior class. Nevertheless, pre-Meiji nomenclature for the martial disciplines betrayed no discernible systematization.

I wish to add that I strongly oppose the claim by some people that it is up to the practitioners and instructors to decide whether they are practicing or teaching *bujutsu* or *budo*. As I stated before, *bujutsu* is the art of fighting or killing. On the other hand, *budo* is the art of living or life—in aikido, it is also called *love*. It is the way that develops and improves the practitioner's character (as taught in the *Dojo Kun* [道場訓]) and helps build principles in his mind. *Budo* enables you to live honestly and righteously, or at least with principles.

Some people are under the misconception that *bujutsu* is superior to or better than *budo*. Perfecting karate skills is the objective in *bujutsu*, and winning a match is most important to them. Since winning is not considered to be the most important factor in *budo*, practitioners of *bujutsu* claim that theirs is the samurai way and thus better.

Certainly, improving karate techniques and skill is a part of training in *budo*, as well—and an important one, too—but, unlike *bujutsu*, it is not the ultimate goal. If the goal of our interest is only winning (killing), then why would we bother learning an ancient and not-so-efficient method such as karate? It is much easier to win (kill) by using more lethal weapons, such as guns or knives. Only in Hong Kong or Hollywood movies can a *karateka* or other martial artist beat up a bunch of enemies with swords and guns.

I have heard anguished comments in the past from many of my students, saying that they could not understand why some of the masters (eighth or ninth *dan*) would do things that were unbecoming of the image of a master. I heard that some of the masters had lied, had dirty dealings with money, and done other unmentionable things.

The students thought that many years of karate training would automatically improve the character of those high-ranking practitioners. They also expected the examination boards of their organizations to have considered the character aspect as one of the requirements for promotion to a high-ranking position. Unfortunately, that has not been the case.

A highly skilled karate practitioner without *budo* discipline is like an Olympic winner who will do whatever it takes to win, including cheating, taking drugs, or bending the rules. This shows clearly that mere physical superiority does not automatically guarantee nonphysical qualities, such as sportsmanship, etiquette, fairness, or respect for competitors, judges, or spectators.

By practicing karate in the *budo* way, you can go beyond physical skills. It teaches you how to be a better person, free from ego, hatred, and wanton desire for money and power. How do you follow the *budo* way? Is it difficult? The answer is yes and no.

It is only a mind-set, so it is not difficult to start and train. But, it is extremely difficult to reach the goal (perfection of character). This is why *budo* is often compared to a religious experience or concept. Actually, in aikido, they have incorporated religious rituals into their training ceremony. It is interesting to note the relationship between the ancient Chinese martial arts (a father of karate) and Buddhism (*bukkyo* [仏教]). The Shaolin Temple is even famous for its role in kung fu training.

There is a good example of the changes that come about when moving from *bujutsu* to *budo* in the well-known seventeenth-century swordsman Musashi Miyamoto (宮本武蔵, c. 1584–1645). He fought more than sixty duels and won them all; thus, he is considered one of the best swordsmen in all of history. However, though he won all of his duels and became very well known, no *daimyo* (大名, 'feudal lord') would ask him to become one of his advisors.

The Warring States period ended in the early seventeenth century, and the feudal lords were no longer looking for good fighters. Miyamoto was considered to be a great swordsman (*bujutsu*) but with no wisdom or vision. He could have continued his dueling on into his forties and, by doing so, could have gained more feathers in his cap, so to speak. But, he decided to turn his art into *budo*.

After he decided to stop fighting—he fought his last duel at the age of thirty-nine—he got into the arts of painting and sculpture, in which he excelled remarkably. In his mid forties, he was retained as an advisor by one of the rulers on the island of Kyushu, Tadatoshi Hosokawa (細川忠利, 1586–1641). He stayed there until he died at the age of sixty-one.

During his last years, he also wrote some famous books, including *Gorin no Sho* (五輪書, '*The Book of Five Rings*'), which proves that he had a great understanding of not only *bujutsu* but also *budo*. Miyamoto was not the only sword master who became an advisor to a feudal lord—Muneyoshi Yagyu (柳生宗厳,

1527–1606), the founder of Shinkage Ryu (新陰流), became an advisor to the shogun—but I bring up Miyamoto here as he is known to Westerners because of his famous book *Gorin no Sho*, which is read by business people and used as a textbook at some famous universities.

By mastering *budo*, a modern-day *budoka* (武道家) may never become a prime minister or president of his country, but people will know that this person has developed immovable courage, unstoppable determination, and firm principles on which to live and die peacefully. He is now free of ego and wanton desire for money and power. He will never be a coward as he has the courage to risk his life for his principles.

We now live in a more peaceful world than that of the sixteenth and seventeenth centuries, but terrorism and robberies are pretty common in big cities. If a robber wants your wallet, it is not wise to risk your life for the sake of a small amount of money. Instead, you will hand over your wallet to the robber, but you will not do this out of cowardice. However, if a robber or a terrorist threatens to kill your family, friends, loved ones, or maybe the passengers on an airplane you happen to be aboard, as a *budo* master, you will risk your life to save them.

I am not totally rejecting tournaments. Participating in a tournament may be an interesting and educational experience for young people or other practitioners who are still searching out the way (*do* [道]). However, I do feel that too much emphasis has been put on tournaments lately around the world, including Japan.

Practitioners and instructors are both knowingly and unknowingly seeking out *bujutsu* while moving away from *budo*. A *shiai* is meant to be an occasion where practitioners can try out their techniques and learn. We need to tell the students that winning and losing matches is secondary. However, karate itself is changing in order to accommodate tournament rules and to win.

Funakoshi Sensei was strongly against tournaments. He feared that the trend I mentioned above would occur. I am afraid his fear is coming true, but there is still hope as we still find many practitioners who wish to go beyond techniques and physical skills.

How do we do it? It is simple: follow Master Funakoshi by exercising the *Dojo Kun*. We must not recite it without meaning it. By reciting it with a sincere desire to follow it, we will internalize it and will finally be able to make it a part of our character. This is as difficult as perfecting karate skills. It may take many years, possibly a lifetime, to achieve. But, I guarantee that you will have a very peaceful life. Once you reach that final goal, you will know how to face death with a smile on your face. That is the essence of *budo*.

CHAPTER THIRTEEN
第十三章

CONTRADICTION IN "KARATE NI SENTE NASHI" AND "SENTE HISSHO"?
「空手に先手無し」と「先手必勝」の矛盾

Memorial stele for Master Funakoshi erected in 2007

There is a popular saying that often goes along with a myth: *Karate ni sente nashi* (空手に先手無し, 'There is no first attack in karate'). Interestingly, although not as popular, there is another saying: *Sente hissho* (先手必勝, 'First attack guarantees victory'). So, why is the saying *Karate ni sente nashi* more well known than *Sente hissho*?

The concept of *Karate ni sente nashi* is supposed to symbolize the defensive aspect of karate. However, many do not understand its true meaning, and quite a few people mistakenly believe that this saying is telling them to always wait until an attack is initiated by the opponent or aggressor and that their first move and even their subsequent moves must only be blocks (defensive moves).

A similar idea to *Karate ni sente nashi* is the concept of *go no sen* (後の先). This concept means that one induces the opponent to make the first move and then leverages that to win the fight. When compared to *Sente hissho*, these two sayings seem to advocate opposite thoughts. So, do these different ideas or concepts really contradict one another?

Let us start with *go no sen*. The short answer to this point is that this tactic or pattern of attack initiative is only one of three tactics or patterns. The other ones are *sen no sen* (先の先) and *sensen no sen* (先々の先). As this is not the main theme of this chapter, I will not go into a full explanation but will only summarize these concepts.

In *go no sen* ('late initiative'), you wait until the opponent moves first. The idea is to entice the opponent into making a certain move or attack that may not be his true wish; thus, his attack will end up being a less effective or uncommitted technique. In *sen no sen* ('simultaneous initiative'), you attack as soon as the opponent initiates his first move and win the fight. In *sensen no sen* ('preemptive initiative'), you sense the opponent's wish to move, and your attack occurs right a the time he determines his intention while his body has not yet moved.

Out of these three tactics or concepts, *sensen no sen* is considered to be the highest level of skill. Therefore, *go no sen* is much less advocated than the other two. If *Sente hissho* is the doctrine, then what does *Karate ni sente nashi* really mean?

Sente is the key word, and it literally means 'first hand'; thus, it gets confused as being a first punch. However, the phrase truly means that a karate person must not instigate fights as he should not choose violent means to settle conflict. This teaching coincides with the fifth *kun* of the *Dojo Kun*: "*Kekki no yu o imashimeru koto*" (血気の勇を戒めること, 'Refrain from violent behavior').

Why did *Karate ni sente nashi* receive more attention than *Sente hissho*, then? It is pretty obvious, and the reader will easily guess the answer. Funakoshi Sensei and Nakayama Sensei were afraid that young, hotheaded karate practitioners would misunderstand the true meaning of *Sente hissho* and take the saying as encouragement or permission to start fights. *Karate ni sente nashi* and *Sente hissho* are contradictory in the literal sense, but they are compatible and rational ideas that apply to the mental aspect of karate training.

Shuseki Shihan Tetsuhiko Asai and Shihan Kousaku Yokota
2005

Printed in Great Britain
by Amazon